IMAGES
of America
HENDERSON

6/3/03

Bill,
It was always comforting to know you were close by in case I blew it.
Thanks for your support!

Dan Kerscher
Rotary President

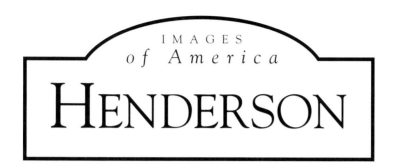

IMAGES of America
HENDERSON

R. Jackson Armstrong-Ingram

Copyright © 2002 by R. Jackson Armstrong-Ingram.
ISBN 0-7385-2087-X

Published by Arcadia Publishing,
an imprint of Tempus Publishing, Inc.
3047 N. Lincoln Ave., Suite 410
Chicago, IL 60657

Printed in Great Britain.

Library of Congress Catalog Card Number: 2002113753

For all general information contact Arcadia Publishing at:
Telephone 843-853-2070
Fax 843-853-0044
E-Mail sales@arcadiapublishing.com

For customer service and orders:
Toll-Free 1-888-313-2665

Visit us on the internet at http://www.arcadiapublishing.com

Contents

Acknowledgments		6
Introduction		7
1.	Building the Plant	9
2.	Working at the Plant	41
3.	Living at the Plant	85
4.	Founding a City	113
Afterword: When was Henderson Incorporated?		127

ACKNOWLEDGMENTS

I wish to thank Joan Kerschner, Director, Henderson District Public Libraries, and her staff for all their assistance and support on this project.

Note on the Photographs

A number of repositories in Nevada hold visual materials related to the history of Henderson. Various federal agencies and private companies ensured that thousands of photographs were taken during Henderson's early years. A particularly extensive collection of their surviving efforts is currently at the Gibson Branch of the Henderson Libraries. All the images presented in this book are drawn from that collection. I look forward to when this collection joins other materials on the history of the city in the archives wing of the library district's planned heritage library.

As the images presented here are around a half-a-century old, they do have imperfections. I have used them without alteration except for sometimes cropping an image that had an excess of background in relation to my preferred central subject. The original photographers, or their employers, often had more interest in capturing buildings than people. But, for us, it is fascinating to get as close as we can to observing the lives of people in our past. Also, it has to be admitted that there is a lot of desert and sky in southern Nevada, and sometimes more of either than was necessary penetrated the photographer's lens.

INTRODUCTION

In 1999 Henderson's population passed that of Reno to make it the second largest city in the state of Nevada. The city continues to grow rapidly and is ranked one of the top retirement destinations in the country. In 2003 this vigorous city celebrates the 50th anniversary of its incorporation. Yet there was never supposed to be such a city at all. This book presents the story of how Henderson came to be and persist.

There are still residents who remember that story and how things looked "way back then." But due to the growth that Henderson has experienced—its founders' children and grandchildren being joined by people from everywhere—there is a need to reach back and reconnect with when the idea of there being a Henderson took root and grew.

There was some small scale mining and the occasional ranch house in the area that is now Henderson from the early 1900s, but the city was really founded on the basis of two previously established communities that housed workers for two of the largest industrial projects in the West: Boulder (later Hoover) Dam, and Basic Magnesium Inc. The two communities would come to need each other for survival.

In 1941 the federal government committed to building a plant for Basic Magnesium Inc. outside Las Vegas where the dam could supply the necessary water and electricity. Many of the workers were housed in a "tent city," and then in temporary houses. They and their families also required other services. A school opened in October 1942, and a hospital in November 1942, along with stores and churches. The establishment of a post office named for Senator Charles B. Henderson improved on the former name of "Basic Townsite."

The bonanza was brief. In November 1944 the federal government halted the production of magnesium and the population decreased rapidly. There was some continued production of other chemicals, but the boom days were over. Like many Nevada boomtowns, it seemed Henderson would likely fade away.

In 1946 the War Assets Administration put the plant and townsite up for sale. Southern Nevada residents persuaded members of the state legislature and Nevada's congressional delegation that Nevada should keep this industrial capacity as it could be used to develop a strong industrial base for the state. Nevada bought the plant and townsite and placed them under the management of the state Colorado River Commission. The residents formed a Henderson Coordinating Council to function as a local government. A Tenants Council was also formed to encourage the CRC to sell homes as most of the residents still rented.

The coordinating council advocated separating the plant and townsite and incorporating the latter as a city. There was doubt about the council's standing to lead this process and the chamber of commerce took over. Many homes were vacant and the Federal Housing Authority and Clark County proposed wrecking the unoccupied areas. The chamber publicized the availability of these inexpensive rental units and the Air Force decided to place 70 Nellis Air Base families in them. Even with this influx, in 1950 the population of Henderson was only 4,000. However, an improvement in the local economy boosted the population to 6,250 by the next year.

As the CRC decided the plant should be placed on the county tax roll to help support local schools, the plant assets were sold to a consortium of the tenants (Basic Management Inc.) in May 1952. Although the initials BMI remain associated with the site, it is important to realize that their use is not connected with the BMI for which the federal government built the plant. BMI in 1942 was a private company in partnership with the federal government; BMI in 1952 was a consortium of private companies that would own and maintain the plant.

In 1953 residents of Pittman and Henderson petitioned the Clark County District Court to incorporate as the City of Henderson. Henderson had originated in the need to house workers for the construction and operation of the BMI defense plant, and Midway City (later Pittman) had grown up on the road between Las Vegas and Boulder City to house workers on the Boulder Dam project. Pittman's fortunes declined after the completion of the dam to revive somewhat from its closeness to the BMI plant. By 1953 it had also suffered from the post-war uncertainties, but it had something necessary for the creation of a city that Henderson lacked: homeowners. A petition to incorporate required signatures from those who were both voters and tax-payers. Most of the housing in Henderson itself was still company owned and most voters were renters. In order to incorporate there had to be a coalition with Pittman.

The City of Henderson was incorporated in 1953 with a population of 7,410 and an area of 14 square miles. Immediately the city set about planning to increase both its land base and population, with population eventually outstripping even the most optimistic forecasts. By 1965 it had reached 16,000; by 1980, 25,000; by 1990, 140,000; and by 2001 the population was 208,000 and the city occupied over 80 square miles.

In the 1970s legislation was passed to rename the city Lake Adair after a planned development around a man-made lake. As the project was not successfully financed, the proposed name change lapsed.

In the 1980s growth was fueled by the development of more successfully financed master planned communities—including retirement ones—with associated golf courses, retail, and medical services. In the early 1990s both large scale shopping malls and "neighborhood" casinos came to Henderson. The increase in population obviously required the building of schools and libraries, and encouraged the development of a park system that in 1999 was awarded the National Gold Medal for Excellence in Park and Recreation Administration. In the late 1990s even the Lake Adair project was successfully resurrected as Lake Las Vegas, one of the most upscale developments in the region, thus capping the rise of Henderson from blue-collar town to American dream city. This book portrays the gritty reality that came before the dream.

One
BUILDING THE PLANT

In the mid-1930s Howard Eells, owner of Basic Refractories in Ohio, acquired mineral rights to high grade deposits of brucite and magnesite—needed to manufacture his patent refractories, bricks to line furnaces—in Gabbs, Nevada. Eells realized that war demand for magnesium increased the potential value of these rights. In 1941 Major Ball of Magnesium Elektron, a British company, was looking for a factory site out of reach of German bombing. Eells persuaded Ball that Nevada was a good location and that his mineral rights would support production. They formed Basic Magnesium Incorporated (BMI) and sought the support of Nevada's congressional delegation.

On July 5, 1941, the Defense Plant Corporation, a subsidiary of the Reconstruction Finance Corporation chaired by former Nevada Senator Charles B. Henderson, signed a contract with BMI to build a plant. The federal government would own the land, buildings, equipment, and magnesium. BMI would manage the operation with the U.S. Treasury meeting the payroll. In September 1941 McNeil Construction of Los Angeles started work.

The size of the plant was much increased during construction and by mid-1942 there were charges of excessive salaries being paid to some executives and war profiteering. In the fall of 1942 Eells sold his interest in BMI to Anaconda Copper Mining Company with federal agreement and Anaconda then managed the project. Obviously, that a few individuals may have exploited early wartime conditions to their personal profit takes nothing from the effort and achievement of the thousands who worked on building and operating the plant.

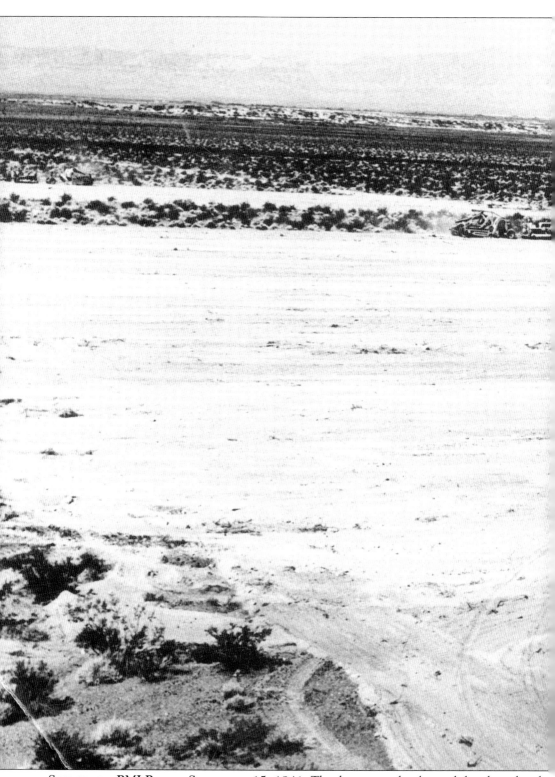

SITE OF THE BMI PLANT, SEPTEMBER 15, 1941. The desert stretches beyond the cleared and

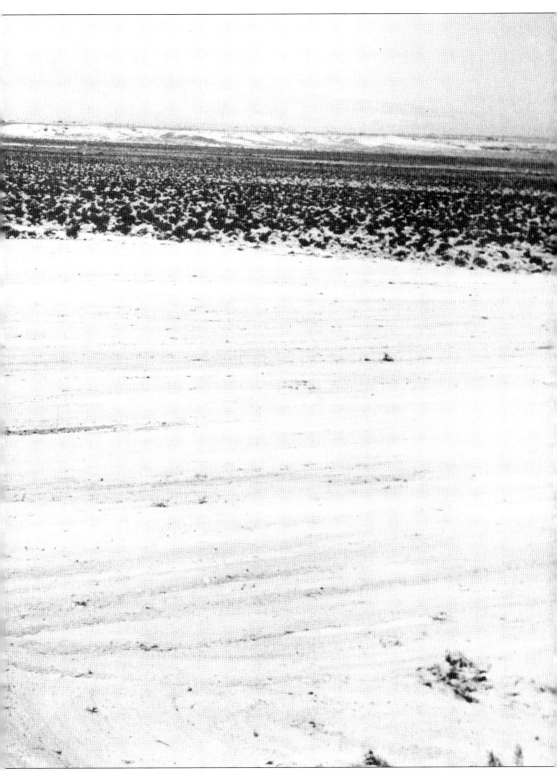
graded site where construction is to begin.

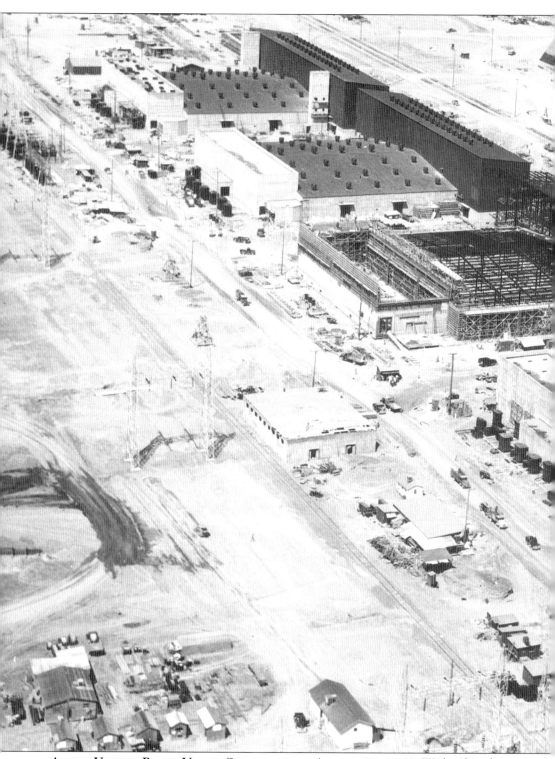

AERIAL VIEW OF PLANT UNDER CONSTRUCTION AUGUST 11, 1942. Within less than a year the vast plant was visible for miles and production of magnesium would begin August 31, 1942,

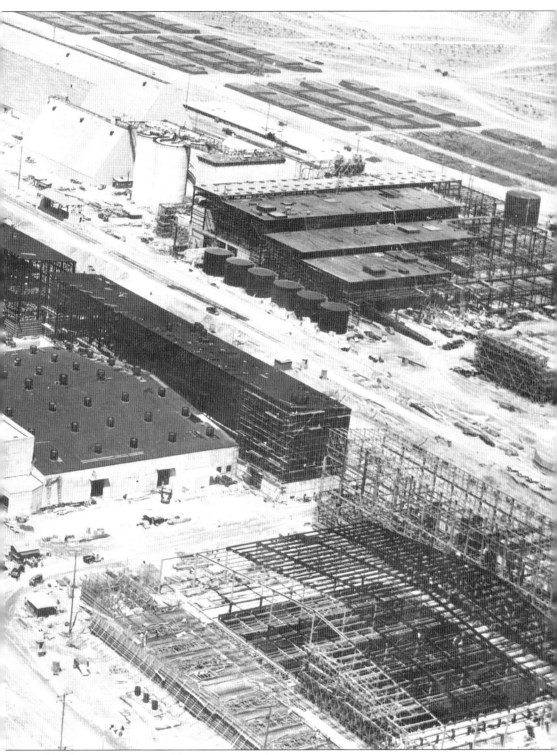
even though construction would continue into the next year.

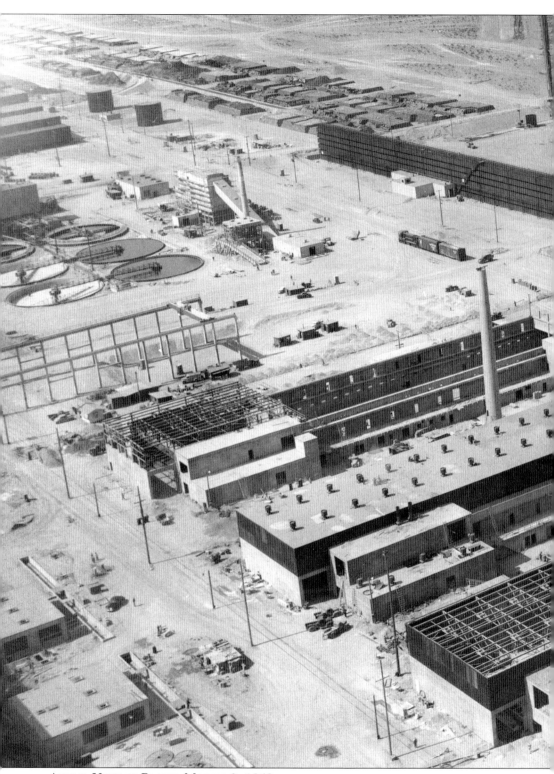

AERIAL VIEW OF PLANT, MARCH 2, 1943.

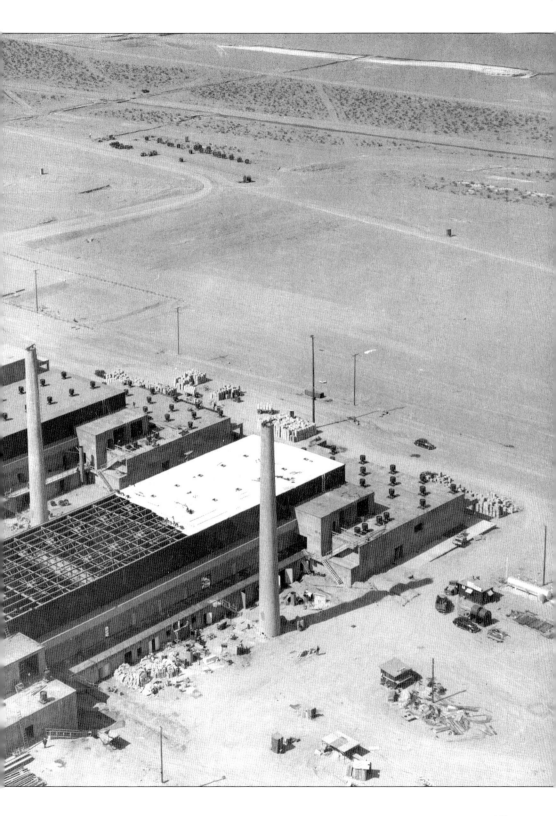

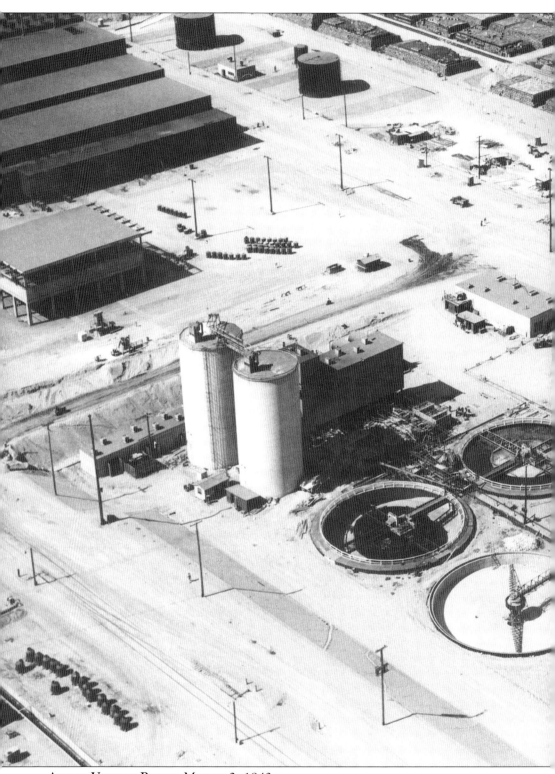

Aerial View of Plant, March 2, 1943.

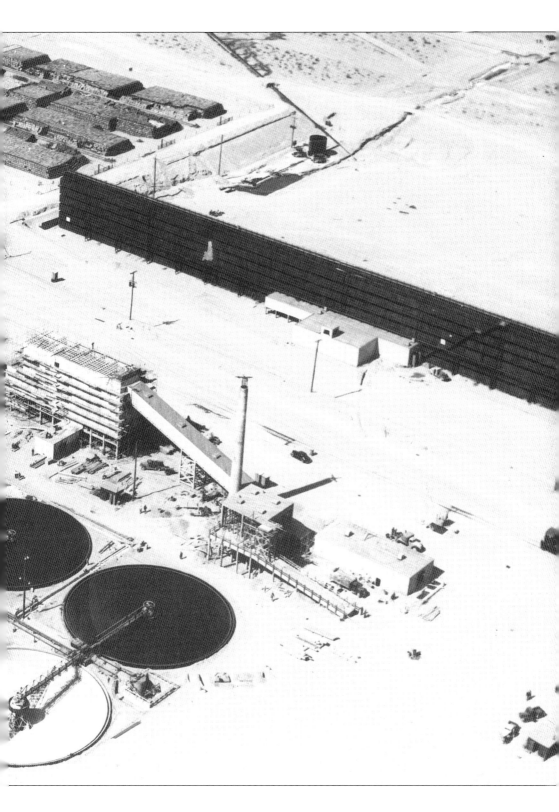

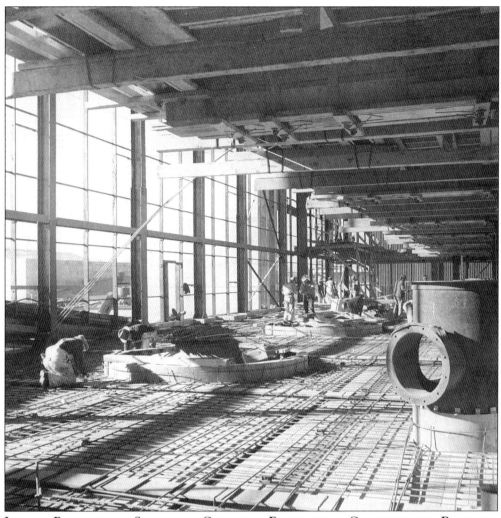

LAYING REINFORCING STEEL FOR CONCRETE FLOOR OF A CHLORINATION BUILDING, JANUARY 1943. Building the plant required 50,000 tons of structural steel.

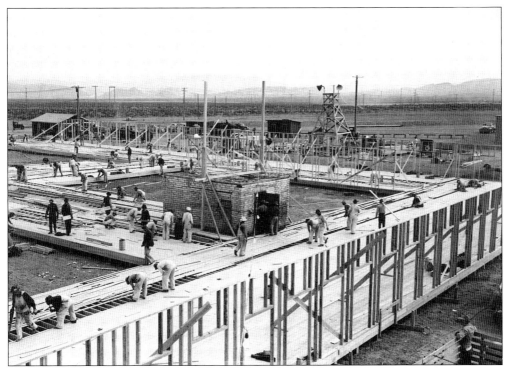
BUILDING THE NEW ADMINISTRATION BUILDING, MARCH 9, 1943. More than 30 million feet of lumber were used in the building of the plant.

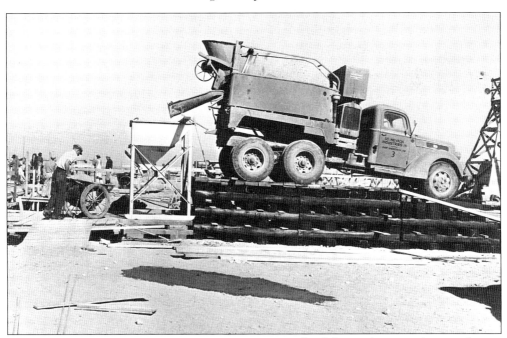
CONCRETE POURING PAD, DECEMBER 17, 1941. Much of the steel was used in reinforcing concrete and much of the lumber in formwork for concrete casting. Here concrete is unloaded into wheelbarrows on its way to the forms.

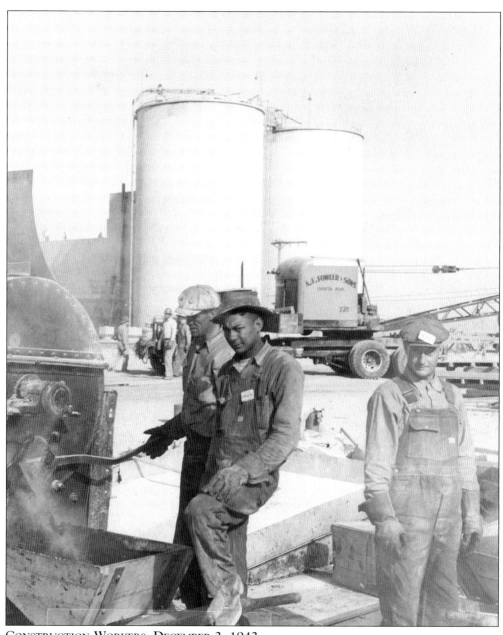
Construction Workers, December 2, 1942.

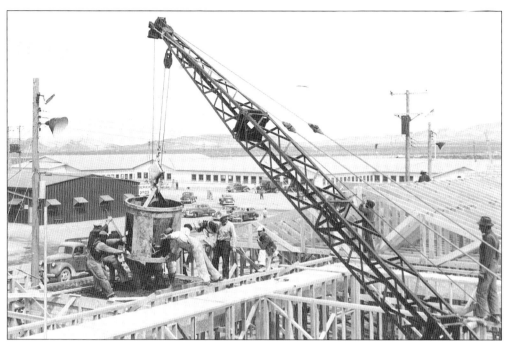

WRESTLING A CONCRETE HOPPER INTO PLACE, MARCH 14, 1942.

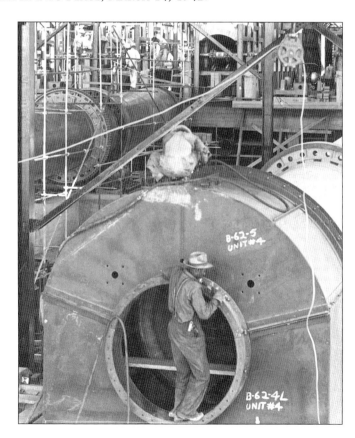

INSTALLING A ROTARY KILN, AUGUST 5, 1942.

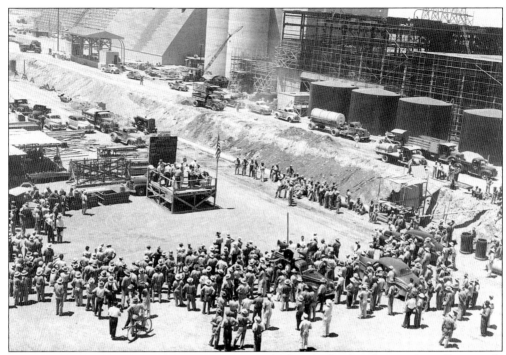

WAR BOND RALLY AT PLANT, JULY 29, 1942. The hundreds of workers at this rally are only a small proportion of the thousands who worked at the site during construction.

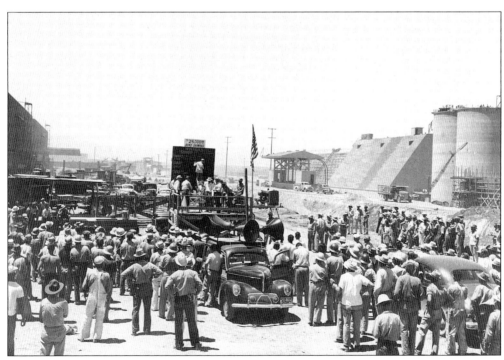

WAR BOND RALLY AT PLANT, JULY 29, 1942.

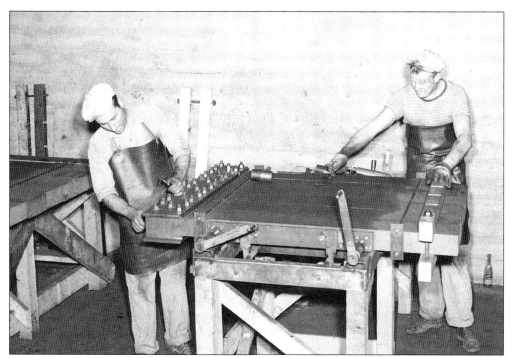

ASSEMBLING AN ANODE, JULY 8, 1942. These workers are assembling an anode using parts fabricated at the plant site. Construction required a great deal of hand fabrication and on-site assembly.

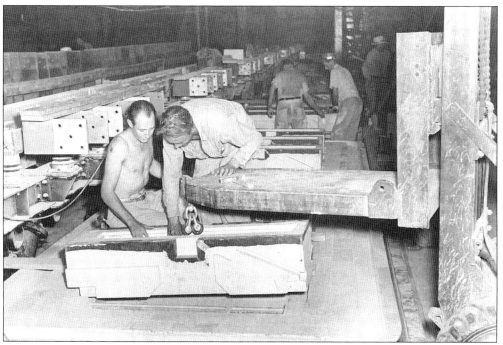

WORKERS ASSEMBLING AN ELECTROLYSIS LINE, AUGUST 4, 1942. The anodes were used in building the electrolysis lines.

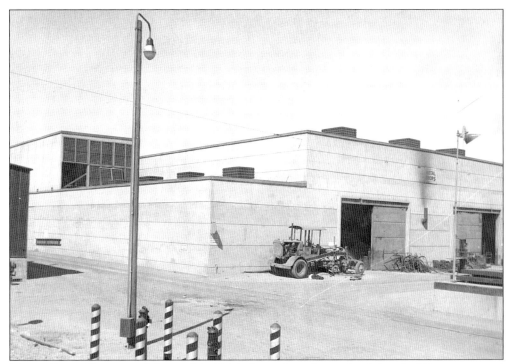

METAL SHOPS BUILDING, MARCH 24, 1944. A number of specialized shop buildings supported construction and maintenance of the plant.

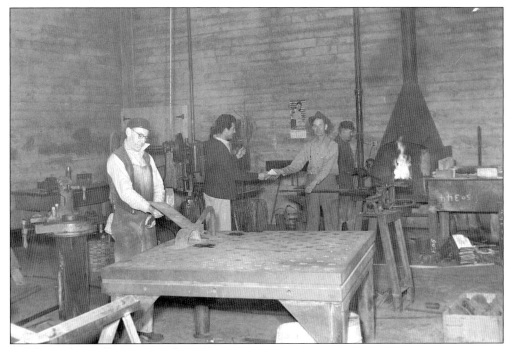

IN METAL SHOP, FEBRUARY 25, 1943.

In Metal Shop, February 25, 1943.

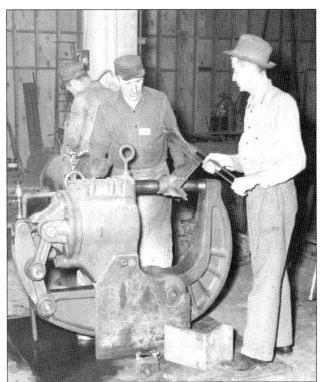

In Sheet Metal Shop, January 21, 1943.

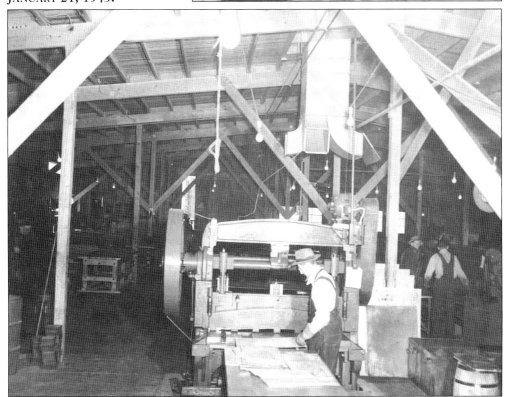

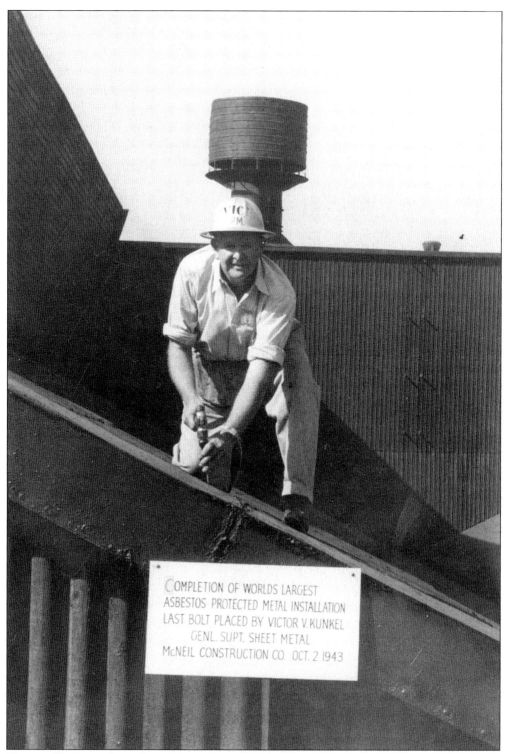

Victor Kunkel, Gen. Supt. Sheet Metal, Places Last Bolt of World's Largest Asbestos Protected Metal Installation, October 2, 1943.

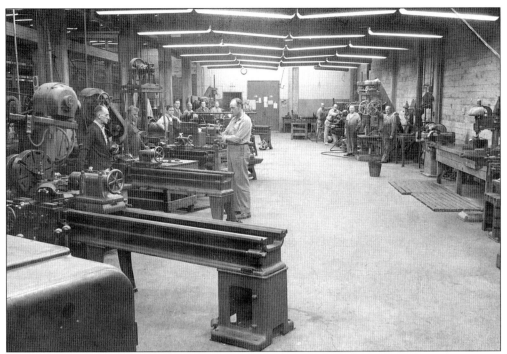

MACHINE SHOP, NOVEMBER 6, 1944.

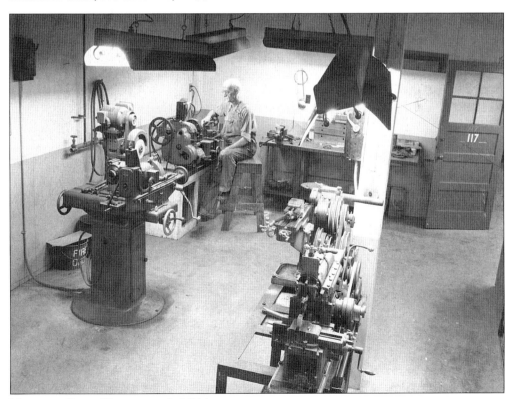

MACHINE SHOP, NOVEMBER 6, 1944.

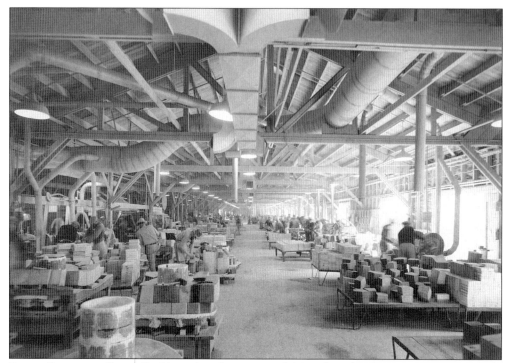

BRICK GRINDING SHED. Building the plant required 20 million bricks costing approximately $15 million. They ranged from common building bricks to special acid and fire resistant refractories. Many bricks had to be custom shaped on site by grinding.

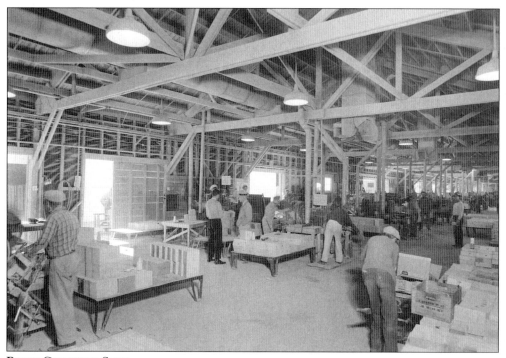

BRICK GRINDING SHED.

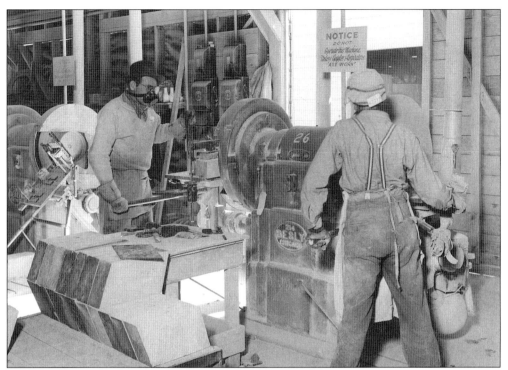

BRICK GRINDING. The notice over the machine reads: "Do Not Operate this Machine Unless Goggles & Respirators are worn."

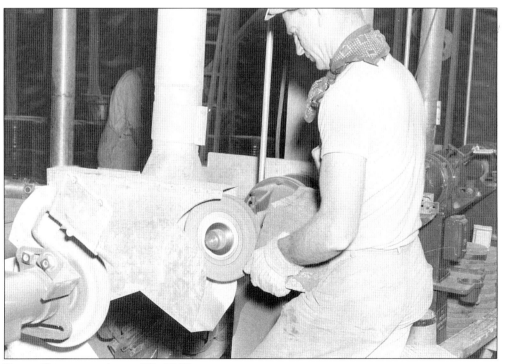

BRICK GRINDING, APRIL 20, 1942.

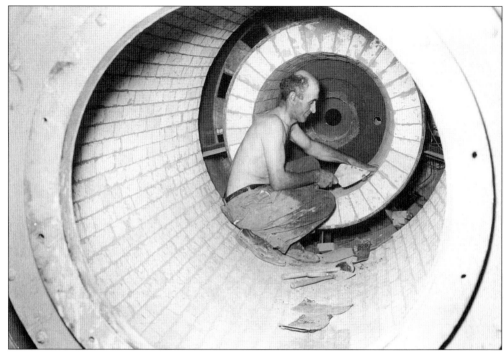

BRICK LAYING, AUGUST 4, 1942. Bricklaying at the plant had its challenges. Many confined spaces had to be lined with brick.

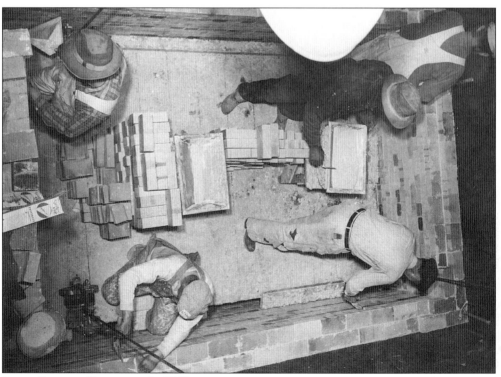

BRICK LAYING, DECEMBER 2, 1942.

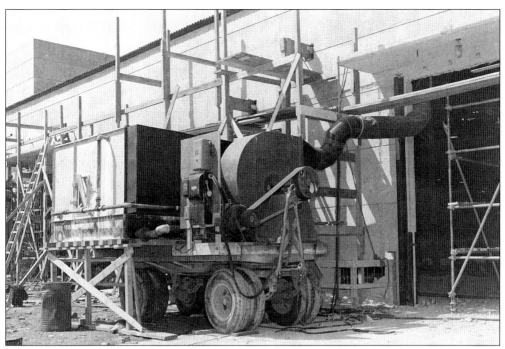

Temporary Venting Unit on an Electrolysis Building, April 13, 1943. A major problem with the plant was that it was based on designs intended for the British climate. The ventilation of many buildings was inadequate for Nevada and a large-scale project to retrofit ventilators was necessary.

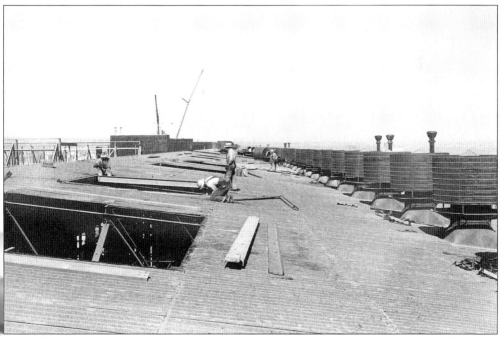

Cutting Openings for Ventilators in Roof of a Chlorinator Building, June 19, 1943. The round structures on the right are newly installed ventilators.

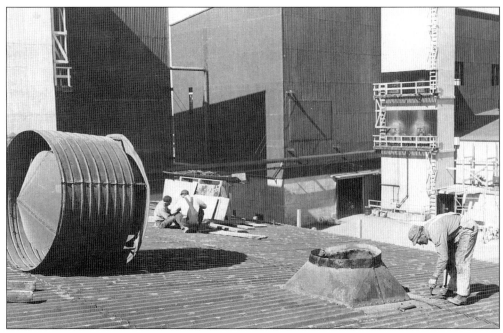

INSTALLING A ROOF VENTILATOR ON AN ELECTROLYSIS BUILDING, APRIL 12, 1943. The ventilator retrofit demonstrated again how such a vast project as the plant ultimately depended on the hand skills of individual workers.

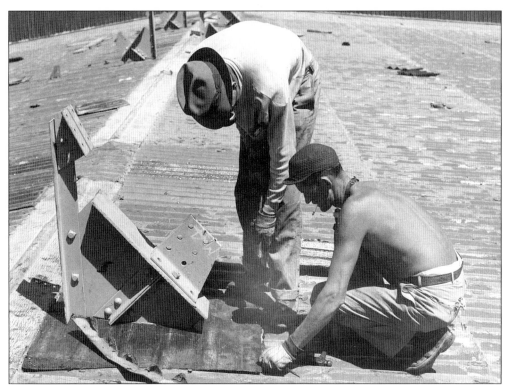

WORKING ON THE BASE FRAME FOR A LARGE MONITOR VENTILATOR, APRIL 27, 1943.

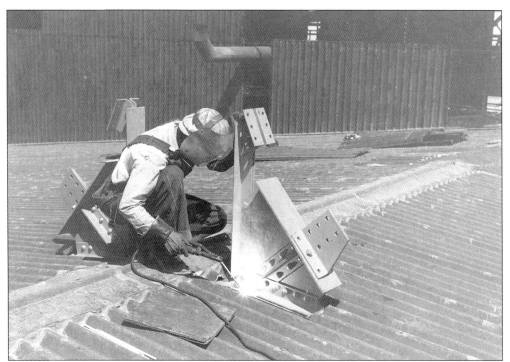

WORKING ON THE BASE FRAME FOR A LARGE MONITOR VENTILATOR MAY 6, 1943. This worker had to endure protective clothing in the desert heat to eventually bring more air to the workers in the electrolysis building beneath him.

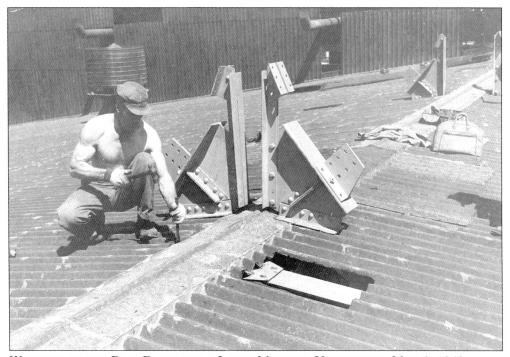

WORKING ON THE BASE FRAME FOR A LARGE MONITOR VENTILATOR, MAY 6, 1943.

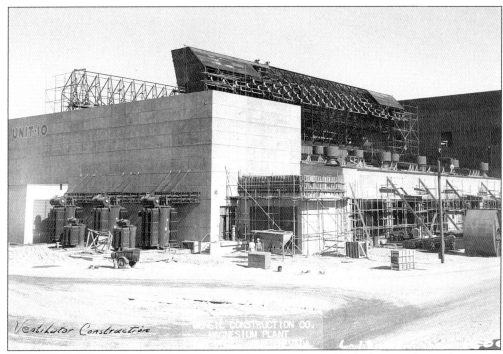

VENTILATOR CONSTRUCTION AT UNIT 10, JUNE 19, 1943. Both the round ventilators and the large ones are being installed on this building.

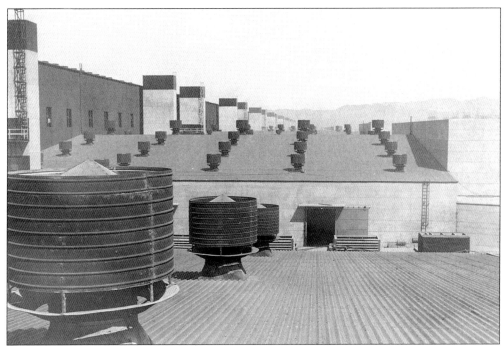

VENTILATORS ON AN ELECTROLYSIS BUILDING, MARCH 30, 1943. The newly installed ranks of ventilators marching across the roofs could only do so much and working conditions were still challenging.

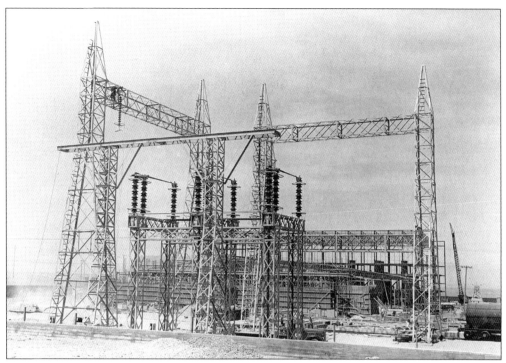

Power Pylons at Plant, April 8, 1942. Plant construction can be seen through the lattice of steel that would support the power lines.

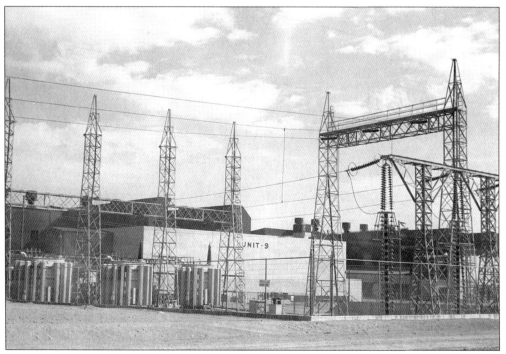

Power Pylons at Plant, September 12, 1944. At full operation, the plant required as much electricity as would have lighted a city of near 2 million inhabitants.

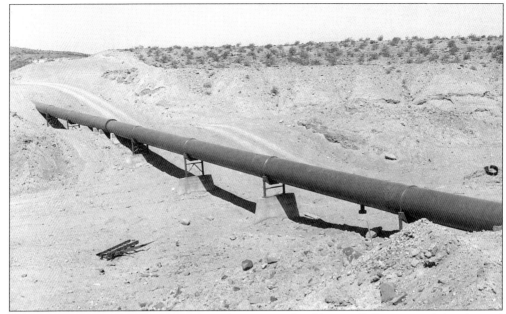

PIPELINE, JUNE 8, 1943. At the urging of prominent Las Vegans, Eells increased the planned diameter of the water pipeline to 40 inches to provide extra capacity for the future needs of Las Vegas. Obtaining ownership of this pipeline was a major factor in southern Nevadans advocating for the state to acquire the plant assets in the late 1940s. Las Vegas drew its first Lake Mead water through a connection to this pipeline in 1955.

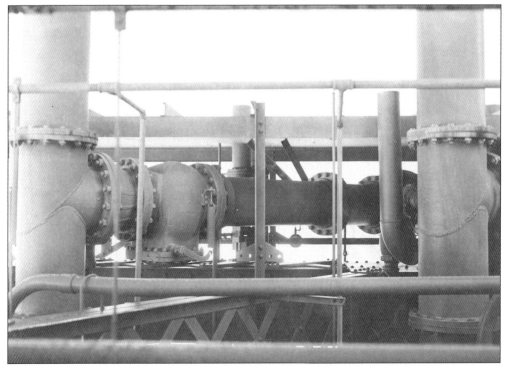

PIPELINE JUNCTION, JUNE 8, 1943.

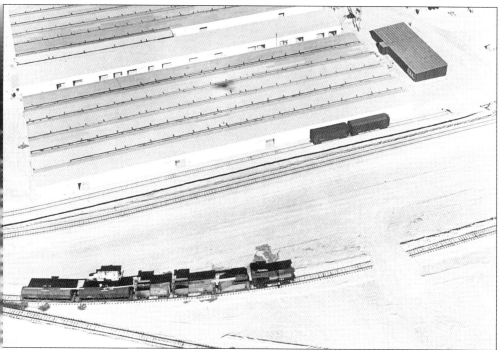

AERIAL VIEW OF RAILROAD LINES AT PLANT, JANUARY 13, 1942. As tons of building materials had to be brought to the site, a spur track was built to connect with the Union Pacific line at Las Vegas.

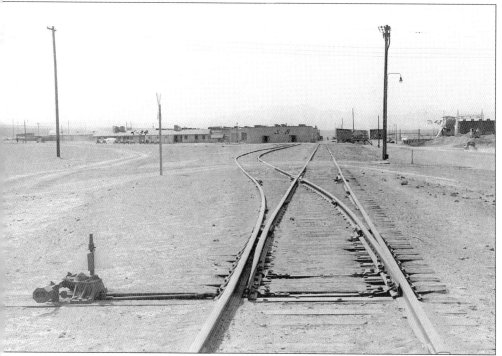

RAILROAD SWITCHYARD AT PLANT, APRIL 3, 1944.

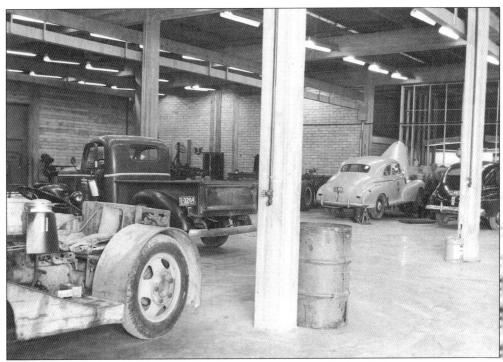

PLANT GARAGE, MAY 10, 1944. The plant's cars and trucks had to be kept in running order.

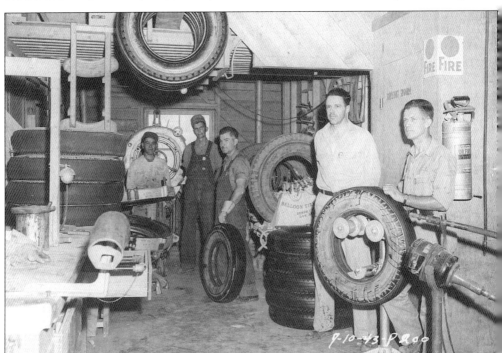

MOULD ROOM AT PLANT TIRE SHOP, JULY 10, 1943. Wartime shortages of tires required getting every possible mile out of each one. Pictured left to right are: Lee Montoya, Lawrence Bracken, Fay Galloway, Mel Oerter (Foreman), and Thomas F. Tweedie.

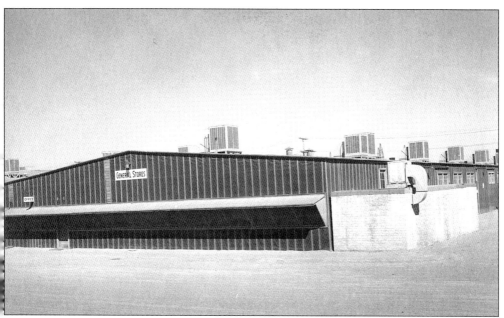

GENERAL STORES, MARCH 25, 1944.

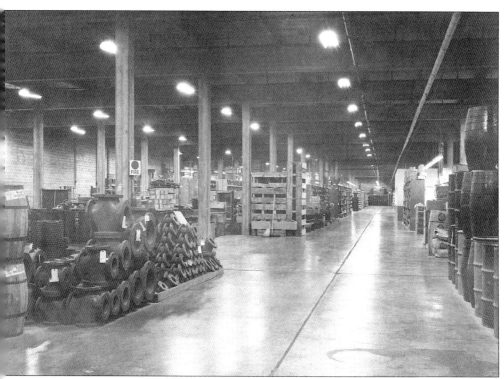

INTERIOR GENERAL STORES. Maintaining the plant required immediate access to a huge array of parts and materials.

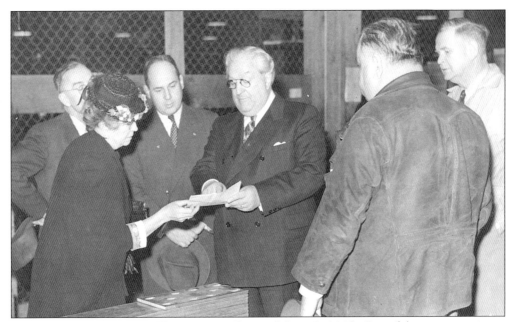

SENATOR PAT MCCARRAN VISITING THE PLANT, MAY 19, 1945. One of the most prominent backers of the BMI project was Senator McCarran shown here (holding the paper) on a plant visit with his wife. In front of Mrs. McCarran is a stack of silver bus bars. Pictured left to right are: Harold Kingsley, Recreational Director; Mrs McCarran; F.O. Case, General Manager, BMI; Senator Pat McCarran; Pop Mohney, Storekeeper, McNeil Construction Co.; and Vic Kunkel, Manager Sheet Metal, Bus Bar Dept., McNeil Construction Co.

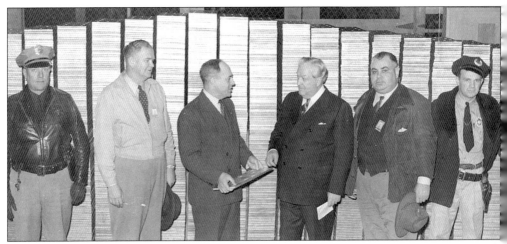

SENATOR PAT MCCARRAN WITH STACKED SILVER BUS BARS AT PLANT, MAY 19, 1945. The plant used six million pounds of copper in constructing the largest bus bar installation in the world. However, this was not enough electrically conductive material, so the federal government loaned more than $23.3 million worth of silver to the project. The silver was cast into bus bars up to 12 feet long to be used in the electrolysis units. After war production of magnesium ceased, the silver had to be returned. Pictured left to right are: unidentified; Vic Kunkel, Manager, Sheet Metal, Bus Bar Dept, McNeil Construction Co.; F.O. Case, General Manager, BMI; Senator Pat McCarran; Pop Mohney, Storekeeper, McNeil Construction Co.; and unidentified.

Two
Working at the Plant

The world-famous "Strip" is not in the city of Las Vegas but has been a vital part of making that city what it is. Even more so, the plant was vital to creating Henderson though it has never come within city boundaries. Working at the plant brought the people who needed the housing and services that would later form the basis of a city. Henderson would never have existed without the BMI plant, and BMI would never have been thought of without Gabbs, or more precisely, Howard Eells' mineral claims at Gabbs. This was not the closest source of ore to the plant, but it was Eells' incentive for the project.

Thus, the first steps in production were the mining and processing of ore at Gabbs. The resulting calcined magnesite was driven over 300 miles to the plant. There it was mixed with coal and peat moss and formed into pellets. These were loaded into electric furnaces called chlorinators and chlorine was pumped in. This produced molten magnesium chloride which was drawn off and processed in electrolytic cells where high voltage caused the magnesium to separate from the chloride. The molten magnesium was ladled off. Later it was refined and cast into ingots ready for shipping.

Magnesium was used for airplane parts, incendiary bombs, and tracer bullets. The first magnesium was produced at the plant on August 31, 1942, and production ceased in November 1944. In just over two years of operation the plant produced 166,322,686 pounds of magnesium, more than the whole world had produced in 1939–1940.

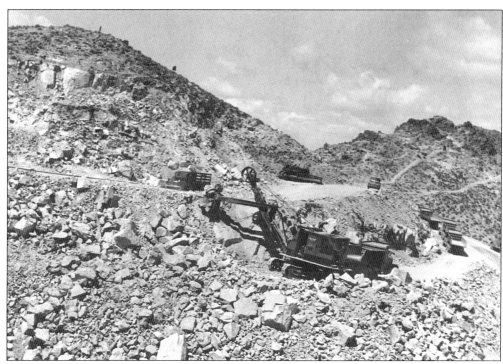

MINING AT GABBS. The ore was mined by drilling and blasting. The rubble was then taken to be processed.

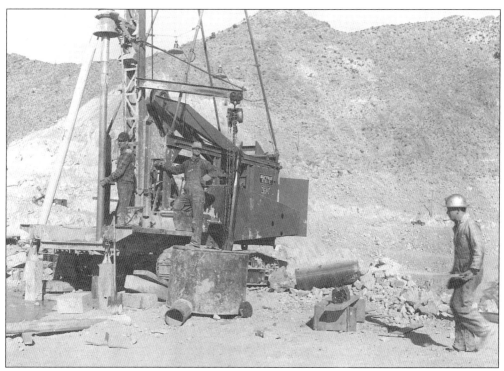

MINING AT GABBS, DECEMBER 23, 1942.

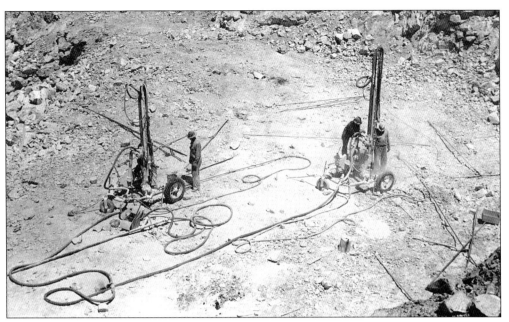
MINING AT GABBS, JUNE 30, 1943.

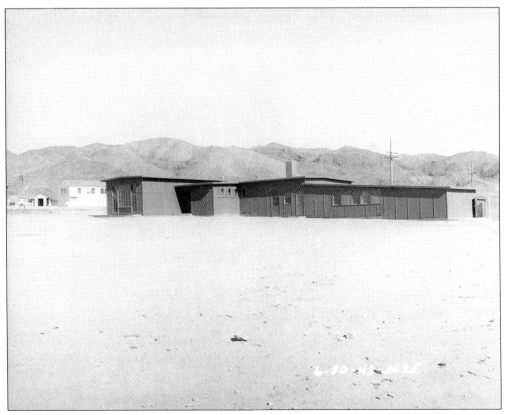
MINE BUILDINGS AT GABBS, JUNE 30, 1943.

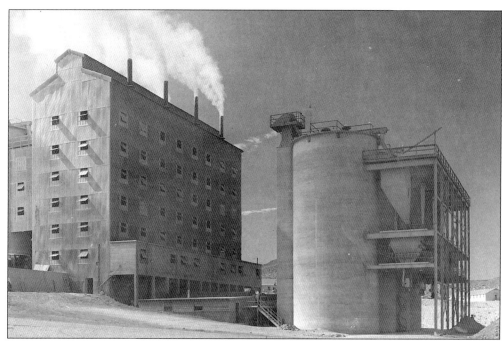

ORE PROCESSING PLANT AT GABBS, JULY 3, 1943. The magnesite ore was processed by crushing and heat into magnesium oxide, or calcined magnesite.

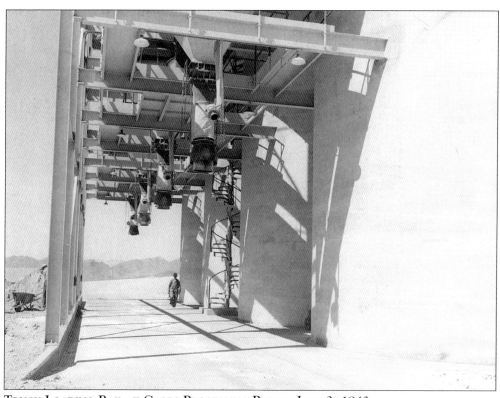

TRUCK LOADING BAY AT GABBS PROCESSING PLANT, JULY 3, 1943.

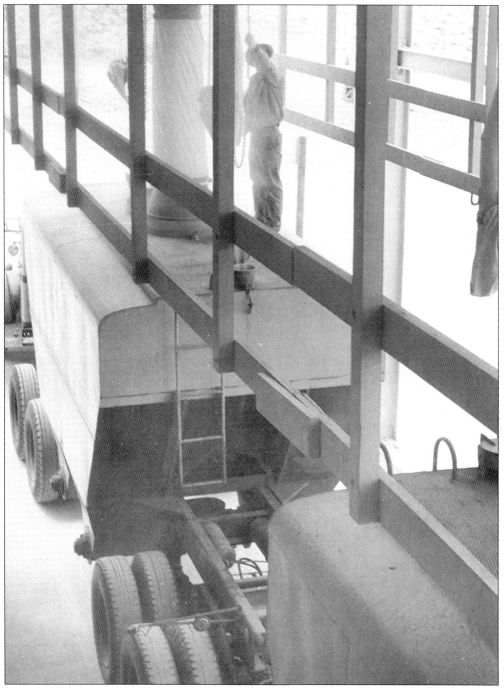

LOADING CALCINED ORE ON TRUCKS AT GABBS, MAY 6, 1944. Specially designed trucks operated by Wells transported the powdery raw material.

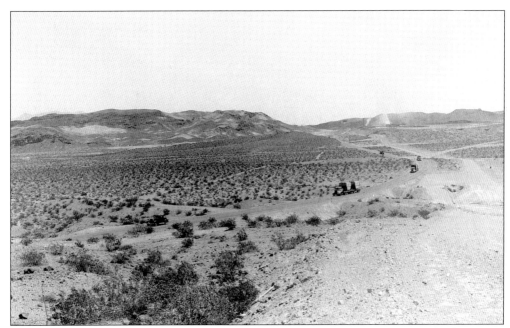

WELLS TRUCKS DRIVING FROM GABBS TO THE PLANT, JUNE 17, 1944. The trucks drove over 300 miles through the desert on Nevada Highway 23 and U.S. Highway 95 from Gabbs to the plant. The federal government not only improved these roads but also built Rancho Road through Las Vegas to keep the trucks off the regular city streets.

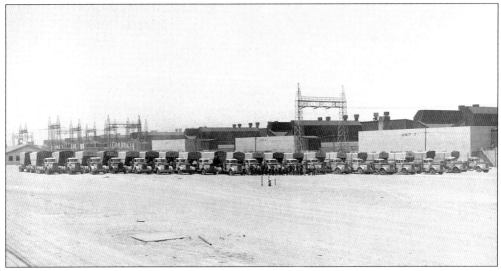

WELLS TRUCKS AND DRIVERS AT THE PLANT, JUNE 17, 1944.

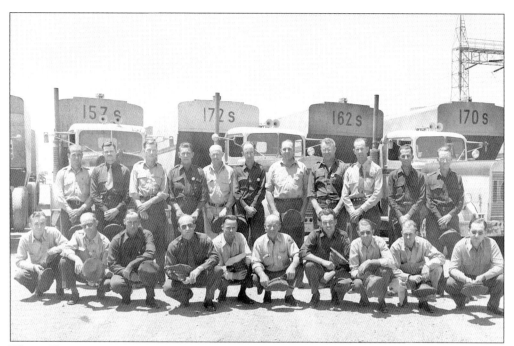

WELLS TRUCKS AND DRIVERS AT THE PLANT, JUNE 17, 1944.

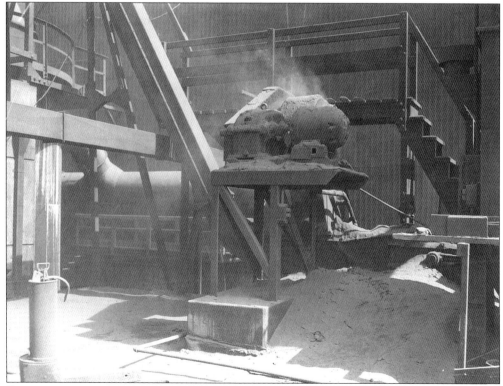

PREPARATION PLANT, OCTOBER 1, 1943. The Wells trucks delivered their loads to the preparation plant.

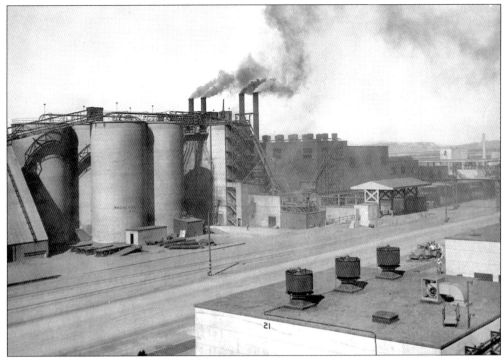

PLANT IN OPERATION, MARCH 23, 1944. In its two years of operation, there was some variation in details of the processes used at the plant. The original process for which the plant had been designed was not the most efficient, and after Anaconda took over management, they introduced improvements where they could. But the basics of the process remained the same: preparation, chlorination, electrolysis, and refining.

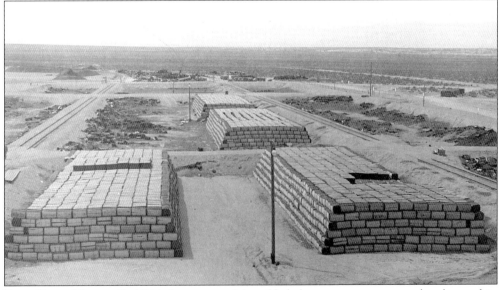

PEAT BEDS, MARCH 3, 1944. Large quantities of baled peat moss were stored to be used in making pellets. The raw material from Gabbs was combined with peat, coal, sodium chloride (salt), and potassium chloride according to various recipes in several types of mixing machines.

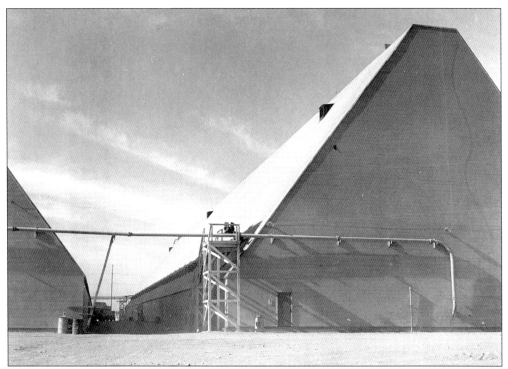

PEAT STORAGE BUILDINGS, JANUARY 1943. Looked at from the end, the shape of these buildings in the desert naturally led to comparisons with the Pyramids. However, the peat storage buildings were 540 feet long and 100 feet wide.

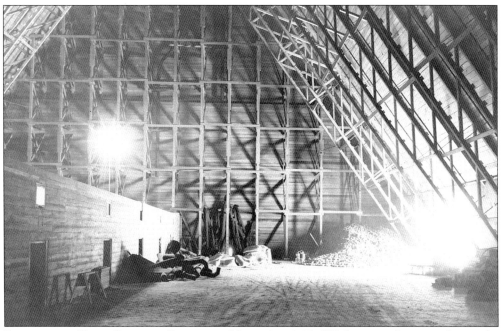

INTERIOR OF PEAT STORAGE BUILDING, MAY 12, 1944. While certainly atmospheric, the interior of a peat storage building was not exactly fit for a pharaoh.

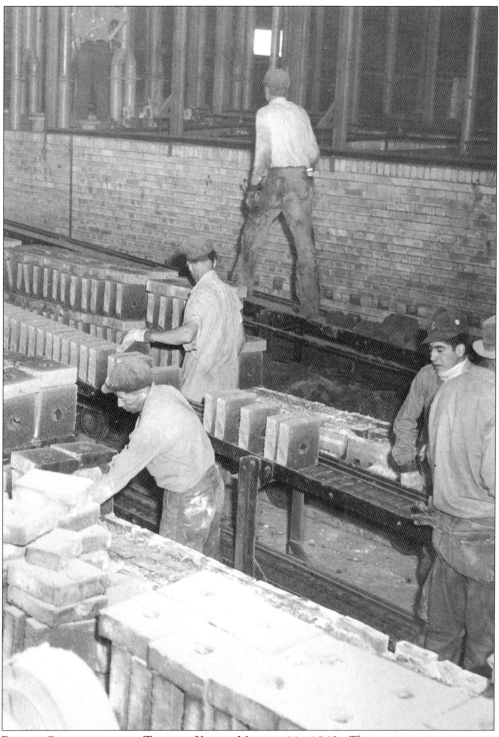

Pellet Conveyors for Tunnel Kilns, March 11, 1943. The various mixtures were further treated and baked into briquettes. These were then broken up into pellets about the size of tennis balls.

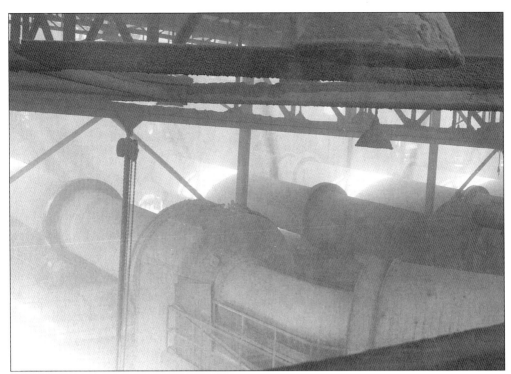

ROTARY KILNS, OCTOBER 16, 1943.

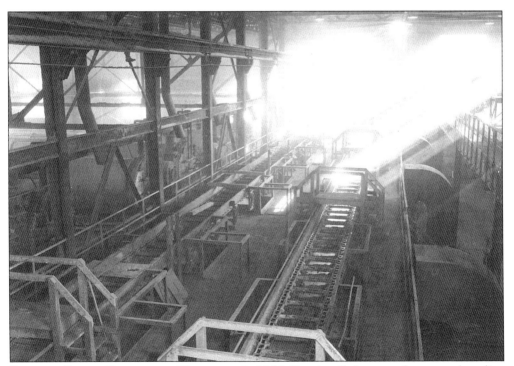

PEATLESS PELLET EQUIPMENT, NOVEMBER 9, 1944. Despite all the peat, there was also a line to make peatless pellets.

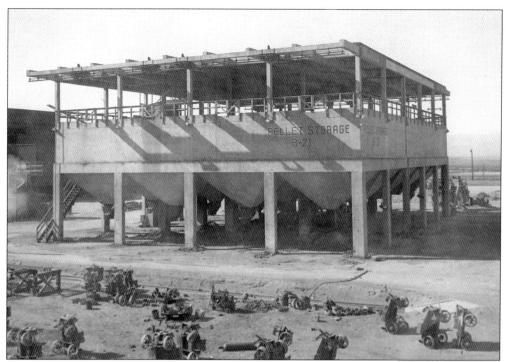

Pellet Storage Building, March 23, 1944.

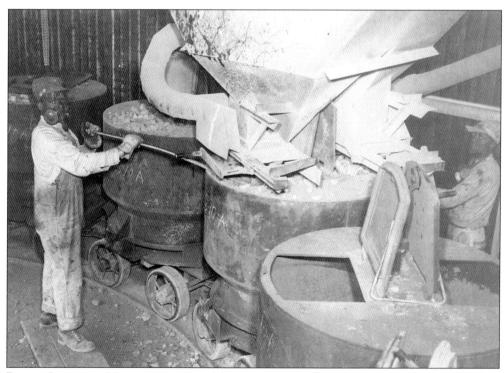

Pellet Loading, March 23, 1944. The next stage in the process was to load pellets into special hoppers, which rested on trailers.

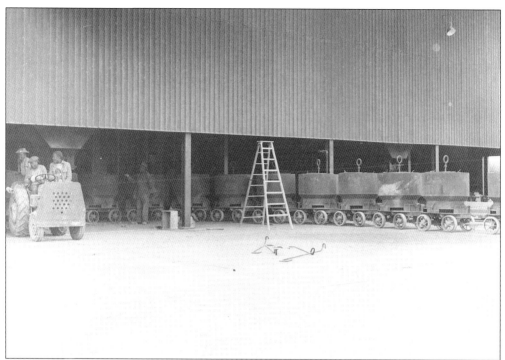

PELLET TRAILERS, FEBRUARY 2, 1943. A trailer carried around a thousand pounds of pellets.

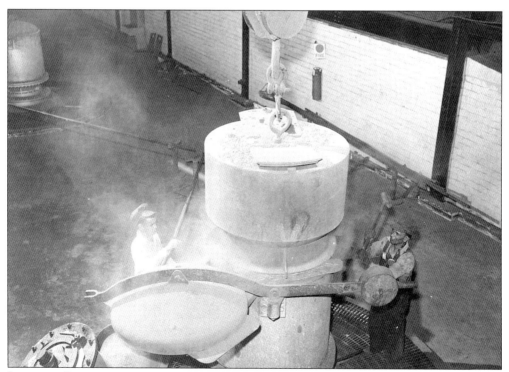

LOADING CHLORINATOR WITH PELLETS, SEPTEMBER 30, 1943. Each hopper was lifted from its trailer and discharged into a chlorinator.

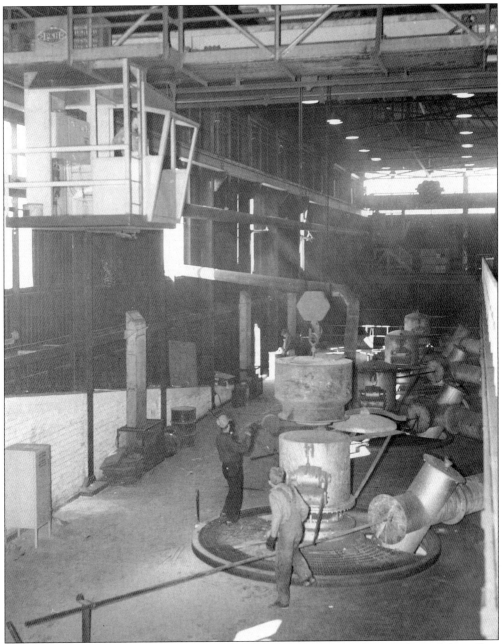

LOADING CHLORINATOR WITH PELLETS, MARCH 25, 1943. These furnaces heated the pellets with chlorine to produce magnesium chloride. They also produced huge quantities of chlorine gas.

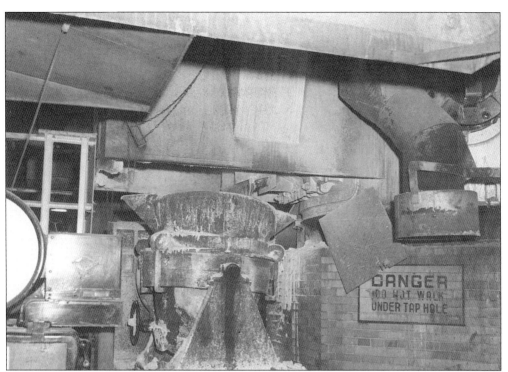

TAPPING CHLORINATOR, MAY 13, 1944. The molten magnesium chloride was tapped into a ladle truck.

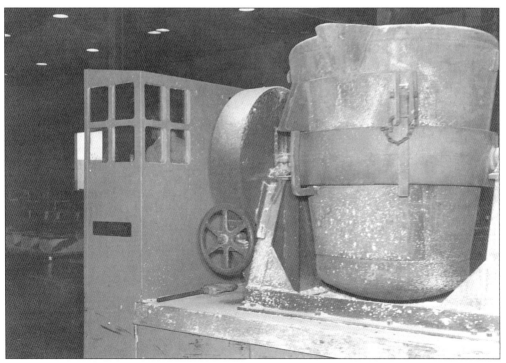

LADLE TRUCK, SEPTEMBER 3, 1942.

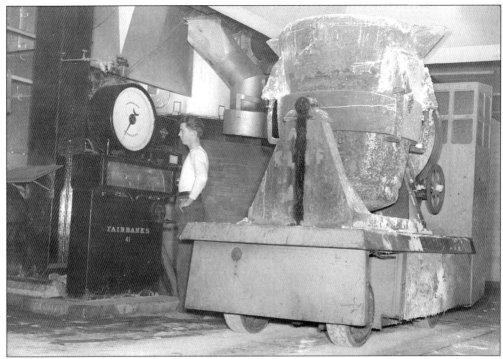

WEIGHING LADLE TRUCK, MARCH 20, 1943.

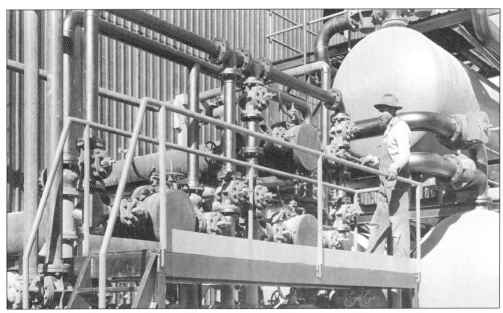

MANIFOLD ON CHLORINE LINES CONTROLLED BY NORDSTROM VALVES AT LIQUEFACTION PLANT NO. 2. Although much of the chlorine gas given off during chlorination escaped into the building and the surrounding area, some was recovered. The plant also directly produced chlorine gas and liquefied it for use at the plant or for shipment in tank cars to industrial customers. The production of chlorine was one of the few plant operations to survive the end of magnesium production.

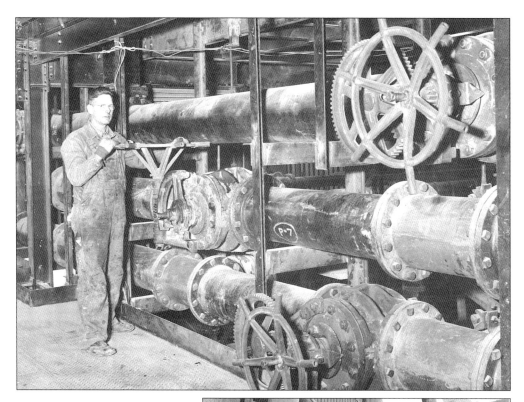

Nordstrom Spur Gear Operated Valves on Main Chlorine Lines in Liquefaction Plant No. 2. With all the corrosive substances being produced, distributed around the plant, used, and recovered, there were extensive systems of pipes and valves to be maintained.

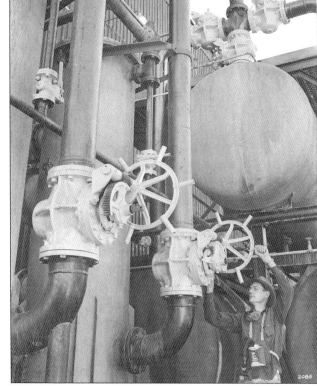

Nordstrom Worm Gear Operated Valves on Sulphuric Acid Lines in Liquefaction Plant No. 1.

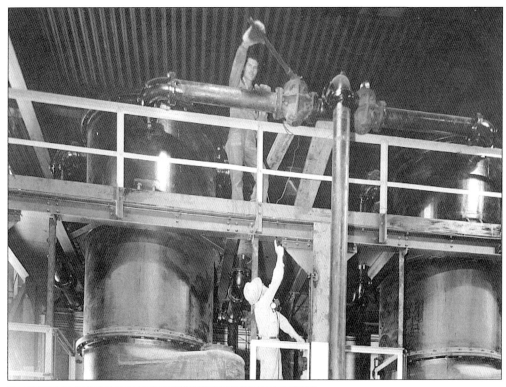

CHLORINE BAG FILTERS IN ELECTROLYSIS BUILDING NO 2. The electrolysis process also produced huge quantities of chlorine gas as a byproduct. The electrolysis cells were designed to assist with recovery of the gas.

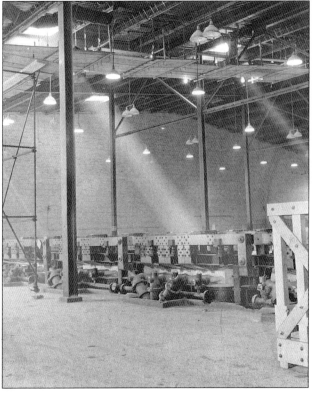

SILVER BUS BAR ASSEMBLY IN ELECTROLYSIS UNIT, APRIL 13, 1943.

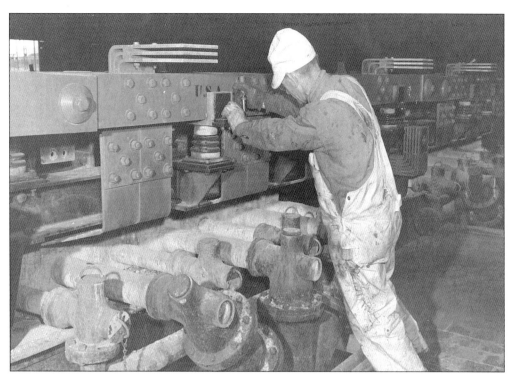

TIGHTENING BOLTS ON SILVER BUS BARS, MAY 2, 1944.

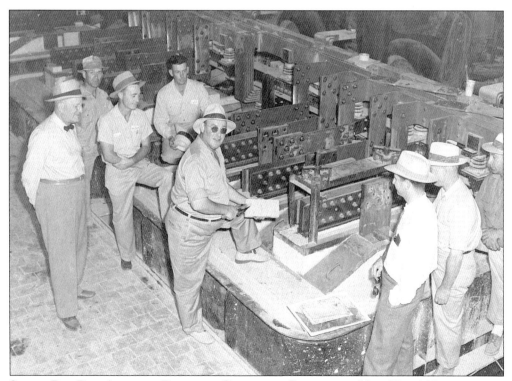

SILVER BUS BAR ASSEMBLY READY TO COME INTO OPERATION, MAY 27, 1943.

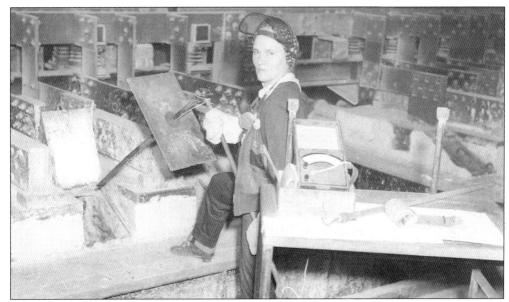

WOMAN WORKING AS CELL TENDER, APRIL 13, 1943. The steel electrolysis units were divided into brick lined cells containing positively charged anodes and negatively charged cathodes. Steel doors allowed access to the anode compartments. The current sent through the bus bars heated electrolytic fluid to over 700 degrees. Cell tenders threw flux into the mixture to put out the frequent small fires and regulated the process.

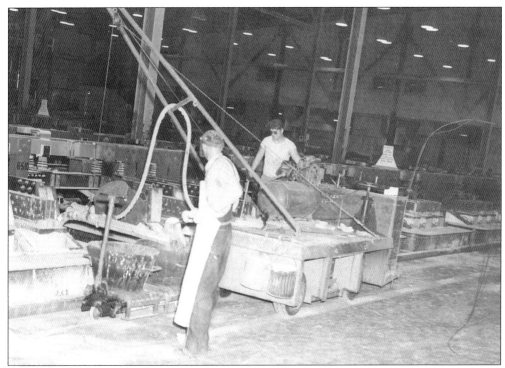

SKIMMING MAGNESIUM, MAY 25, 1943. As the magnesium separated from the chloride it was skimmed off as magnesium "cheesecakes."

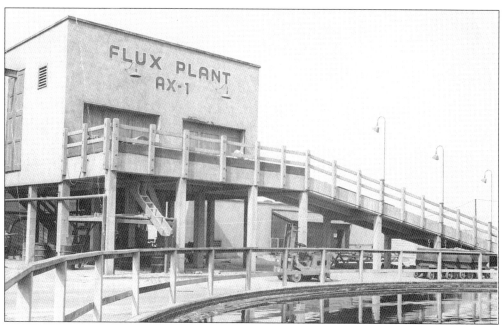

FLUX PLANT, SEPTEMBER 1, 1944. The liquid in front of the Flux Plant is one of the neutralization tanks.

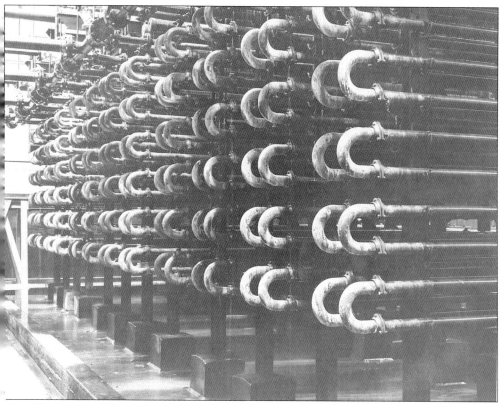

ACID RECOVERY, MAY 1, 1944.

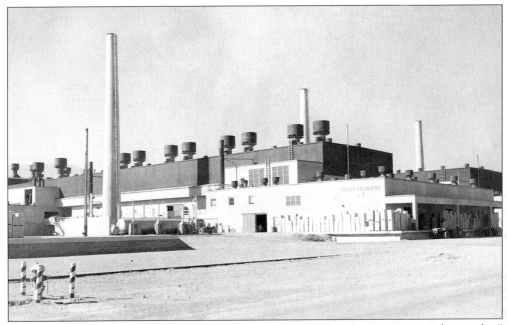

INGOT FOUNDRY, MARCH 24, 1944. The final step was to refine the magnesium "cheesecakes" and cast the pure or alloyed magnesium into bars, ingots, or other forms.

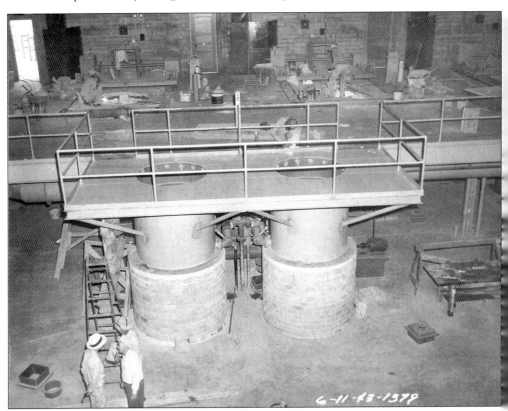

CRUCIBLE COOLING UNIT IN REFINERY, JUNE 11, 1943.

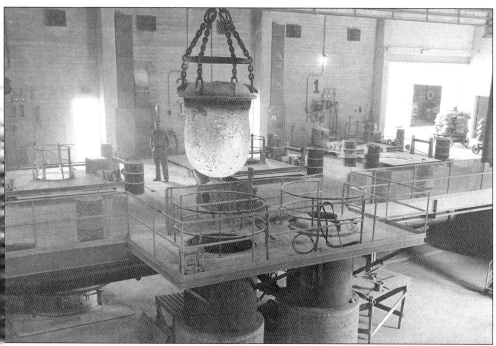

CRUCIBLE OF MOLTEN METAL BEING LOWERED INTO COOLER.

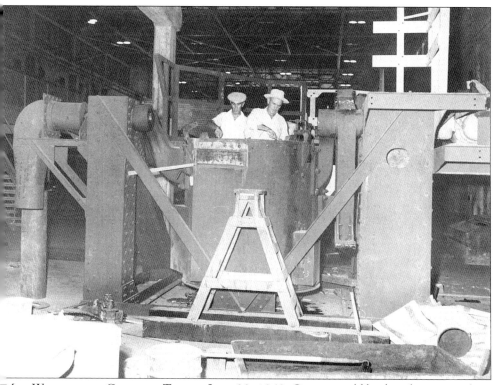

MEN WORKING ON CRUCIBLE TILTER, JULY 29, 1943. Casting could be done by pouring from a large crucible held in a crucible tilter.

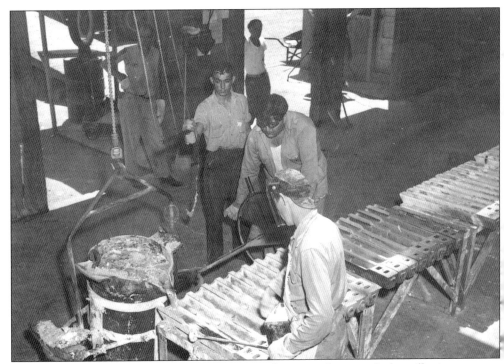

CASTING INGOTS JUNE 11, 1943. Here ingots are being cast by a simple, but effective, process. The hoist operator (David Chasten) positions the ladle of molten metal. Another worker (H.F. Tyranski) turns the handle to pour the metal. And a third worker (Edward Shipman) sulphurs.

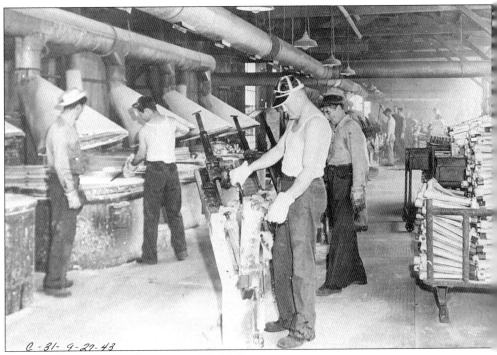

CASTING PRODUCTION, SEPTEMBER 27, 1943.

STACKING NEWLY CAST INGOTS, FEBRUARY 1943. Oversized asbestos mittens are used to handle the hot ingots.

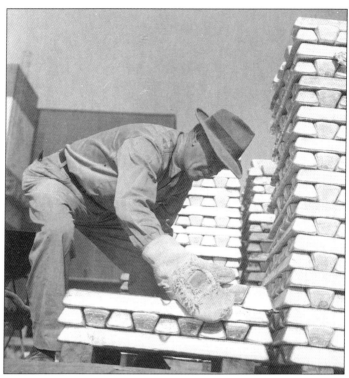

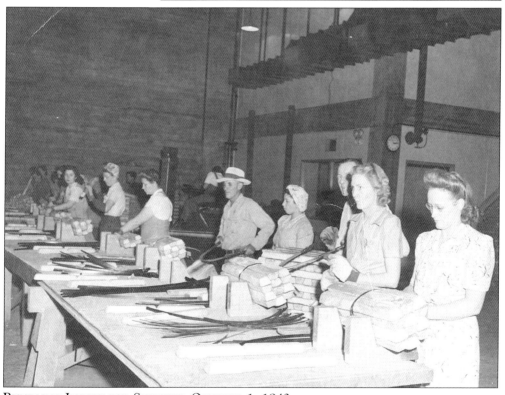

BUNDLING INGOTS FOR SHIPPING, OCTOBER 1, 1943.

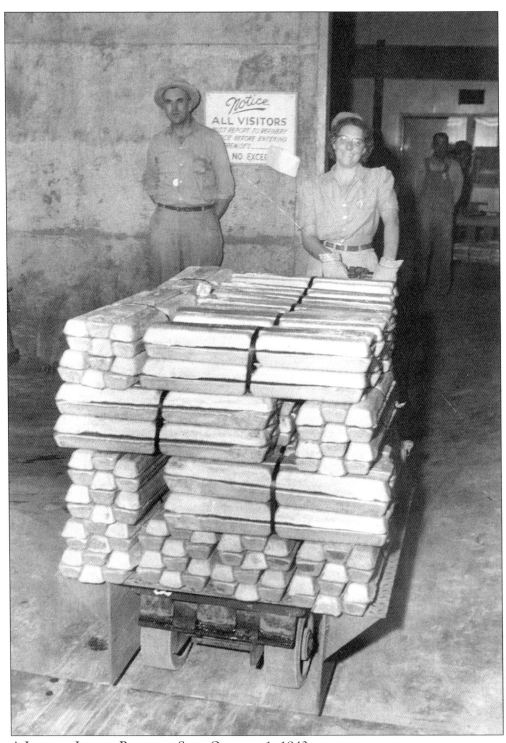

A LOAD OF INGOTS READY TO SHIP, OCTOBER 1, 1943.

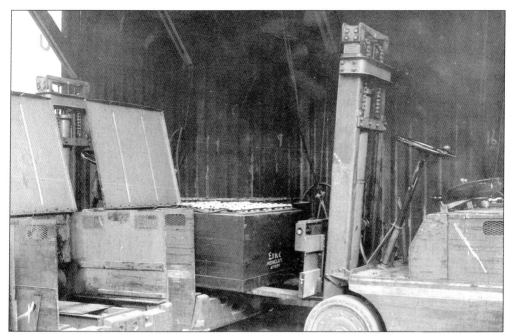

FORKLIFT TRUCK CHANGING BATTERY IN ANOTHER FORKLIFT TRUCK, DECEMBER 14, 1944. The specialized trucks that were used inside the plant—forklift trucks, ladle trucks, pellet trucks—were powered by electric batteries.

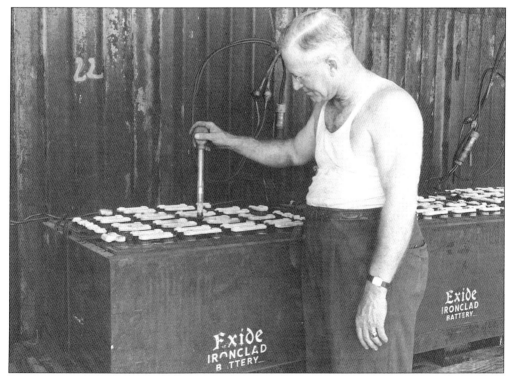

RECHARGING AND SERVICING ELECTRIC STORAGE BATTERIES, JUNE 12, 1944.

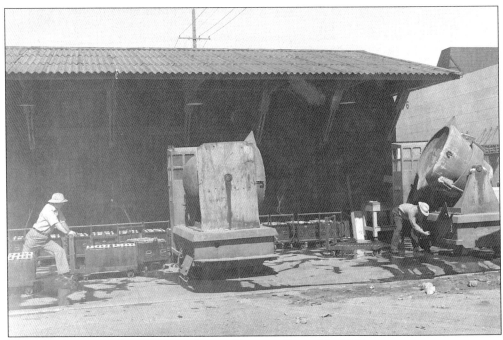

PUTTING CHARGED BATTERIES IN LADLE TRUCKS, JUNE 13, 1944.

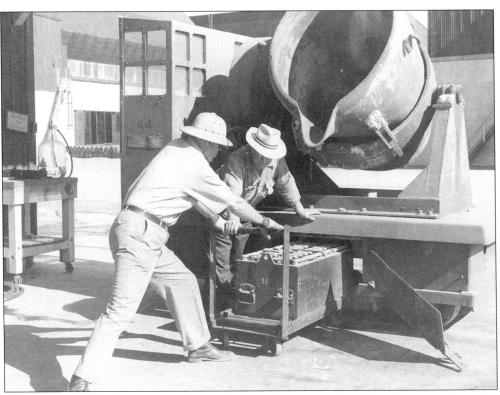

PUTTING CHARGED BATTERY IN LADLE TRUCK, JUNE 13, 1944. The little sign above the table at the left says: "Ring Bell for Battery."

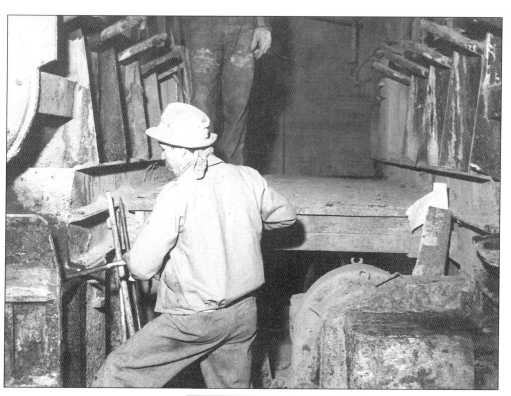

Plant Worker, November 11, 1943. Working conditions in many parts of the plant were harsh, dirty, and dangerous with confined spaces, toxic fumes, scalding brews, and summer temperatures often much over 100 degrees.

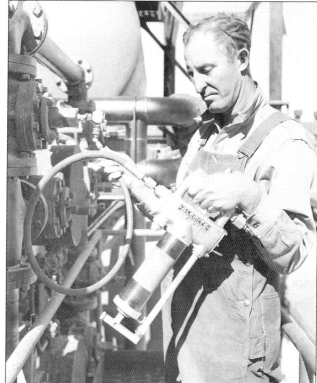

Performing Pressure Tests. Not all plant jobs were as dirty as working on the production line. Many support positions were needed to keep the lines operating.

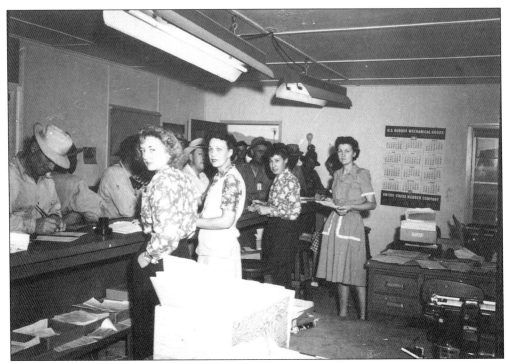

PLANT OFFICE WORKERS, JULY 14, 1943.

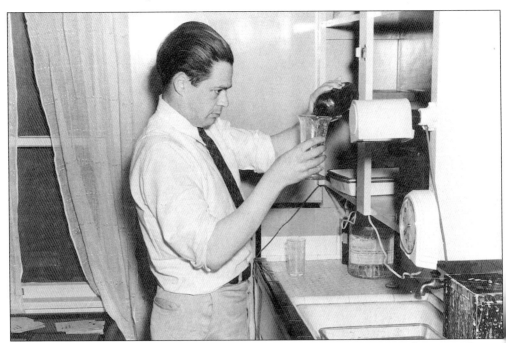

PHOTOGRAPHY LAB, MARCH 9, 1942. Although many official photographs were taken of plant construction, judging from the residential décor in the backgrounds of these shots of darkroom work, the photographers were not accommodated at the plant—or at least not by March 1942.

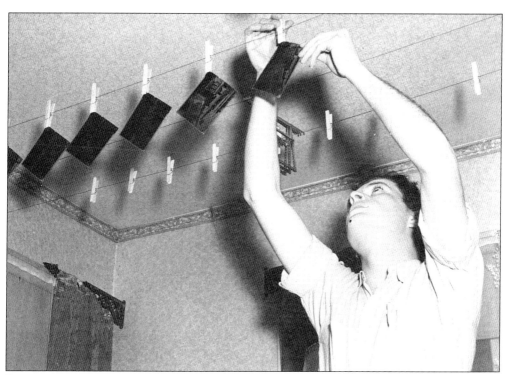

PHOTOGRAPHY LAB, MARCH 10, 1942.

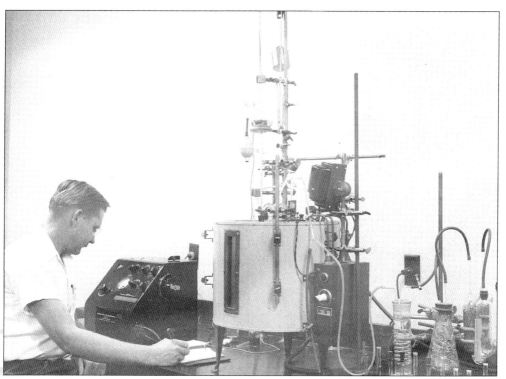

TECH LAB, NOVEMBER 12, 1943. The plant had a fully equipped technical laboratory.

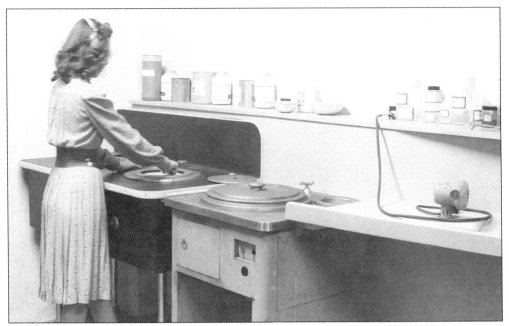

Tech Lab, November 12, 1943.

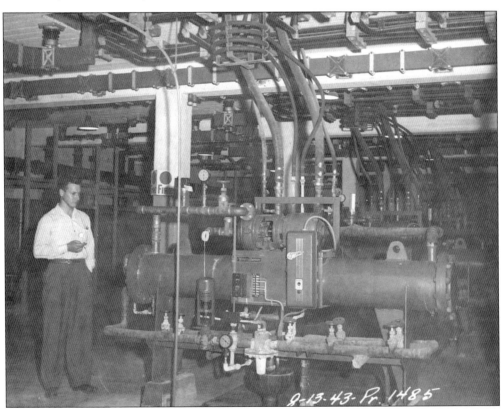

Rectifier Heat Exchanger, August 13, 1943. Many pieces of equipment throughout the plant required the attention of specialized engineering staff.

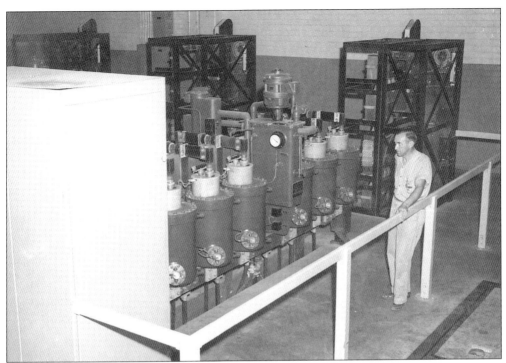
MERCURY VAPOR RECTIFIERS, AUGUST 13, 1943.

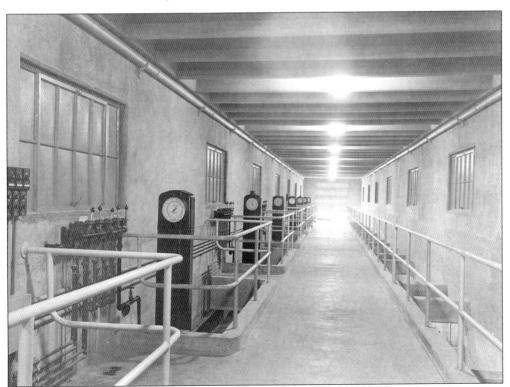
FILTER PIPE GALLERY, FEBRUARY 16, 1944.

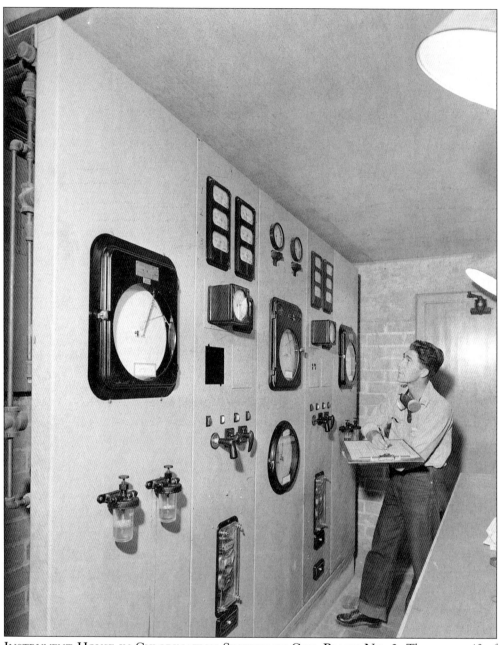

INSTRUMENT HOUSE IN CHLORINATION SECTION OF CELL PLANT NO. 2. There were 40 of these instrument houses.

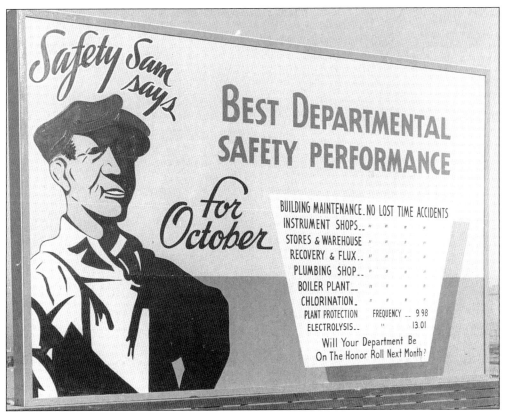

SAFETY PERFORMANCE SIGN NOVEMBER 11, 1943. With difficult working conditions and a rapid workforce turnover, the plant emphasized the positive wherever it could, as with this safety performance sign.

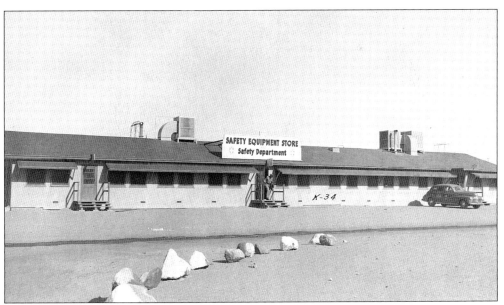

FIRST AID AND SAFETY DEPARTMENT MARCH 23, 1944.

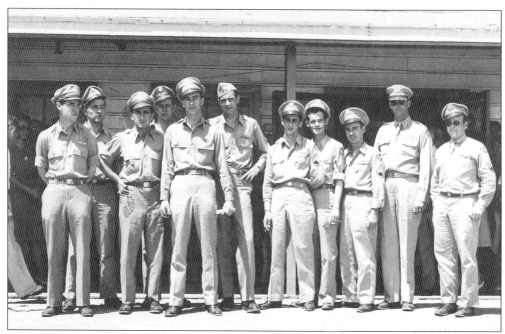

MEMPHIS BELLE CREW MEMBERS VISITING PLANT, JULY 13, 1943. The *Memphis Belle* was a B17 Flying Fortress that was retired after 25 successful bombing missions and sent on a tour of Army Air Force training bases in the U.S. beginning in July 1943. Pictured left to right are: Capt. Charles B. Leighton (navigator), Tech Sgt. Harold Loch, Capt. James A. Verinis, Sgt. Robert J. Hanson (radio operator), Capt. Vincent B. Evans (bombardier), Maj. Robert K. Morgan (pilot), Staff Sgt. Casimer A. Nastal (right waist gunner), unidentified, Staff Sgt. Cecil H. Scott (ball turret gunner), unidentified, and Staff Sgt. John D. Quinlan (tail gunner).

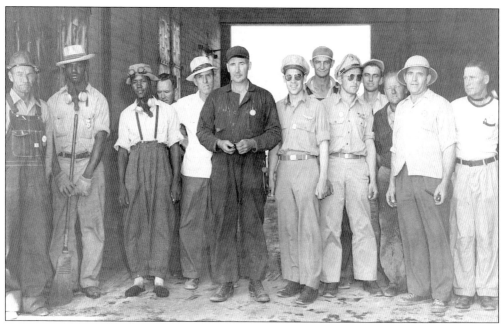

MEMPHIS BELLE CREW MEMBERS WITH PLANT WORKERS, JULY 13, 1943.

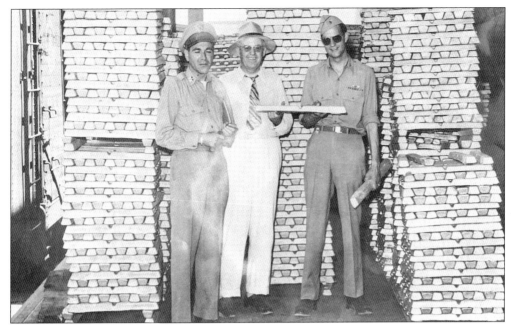

MEMPHIS BELLE CREW MEMBERS WITH MAGNESIUM INGOTS, JULY 13, 1943. Pictured left to right are: Capt. Charles B. Leighton, unidentified, and Maj. Robert K. Morgan.

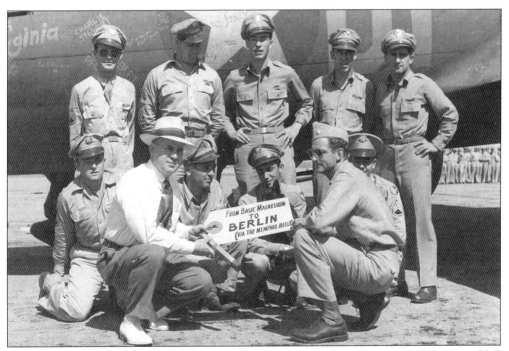

MEMPHIS BELLE CREW MEMBERS WITH PLANT MANAGER, JULY 13, 1943. F.O. Case, BMI General Manager, and Maj. Robert K. Morgan hold a labeled "match." Behind them are, left to right: (front row) Staff Sgt. John P. Quinlan, Tech Sgt. Harold F. Loch, Staff Sgt. Casimer A. Nastal, and Staff Sgt. Cecil H. Scott; (back row) Staff Sgt. Clarence E. Winchell, Sgt. Robert J. Hanson, Capt. Vincent B. Evans, Capt. Charles B. Leighton, and Capt. James A. Verinis.

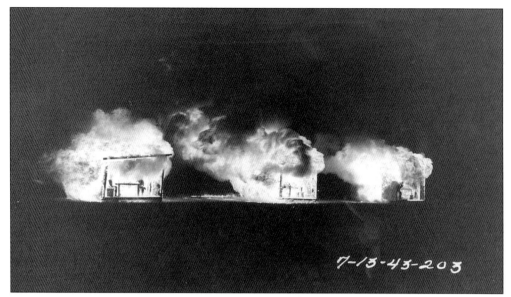

INCENDIARY BOMB DEMONSTRATION, JULY 13, 1943. Magnesium was used in making incendiary bombs such as the ones used for this demonstration.

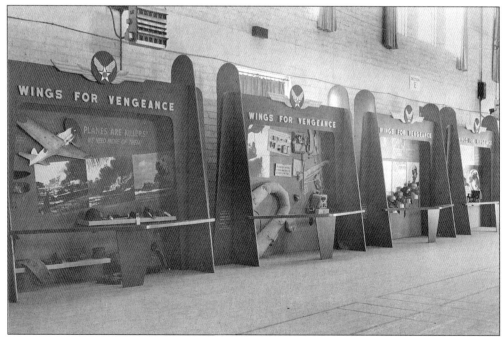

PANELS AT AVIADA EXHIBIT, APRIL 15, 1944. This traveling exhibit showcased the importance of the Army Air Corps to the war effort.

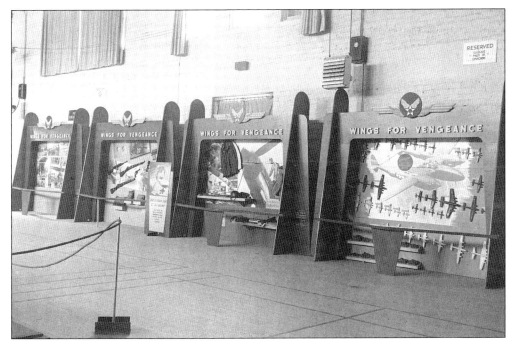
Panels at Aviada Exhibit, April 15, 1944.

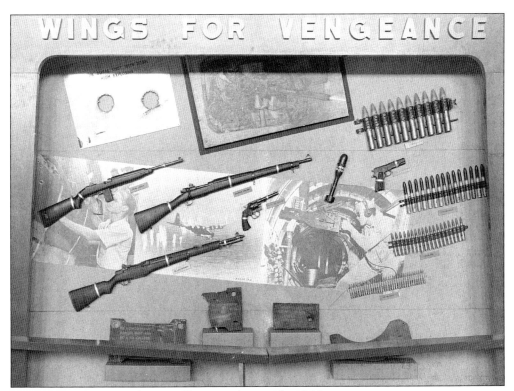
Details of Panel at Aviada Exhibit, April 15, 1944.

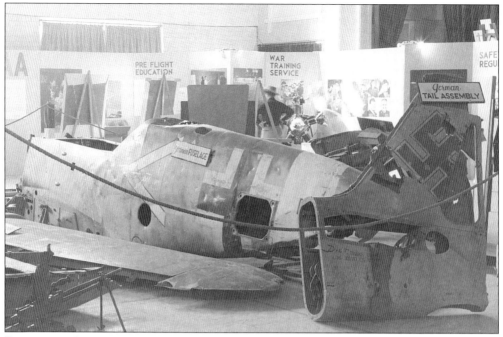

Display at Aviada Exhibit, April 15, 1944.

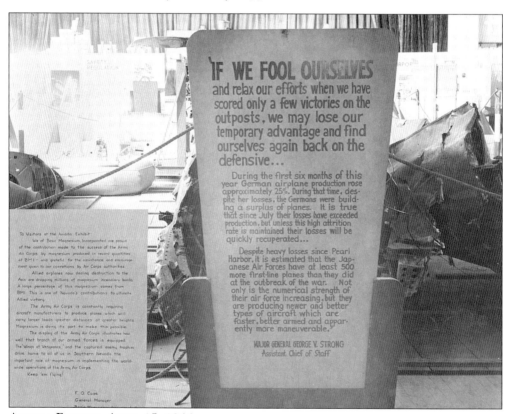

Aviada Exhibit, April 15, 1944.

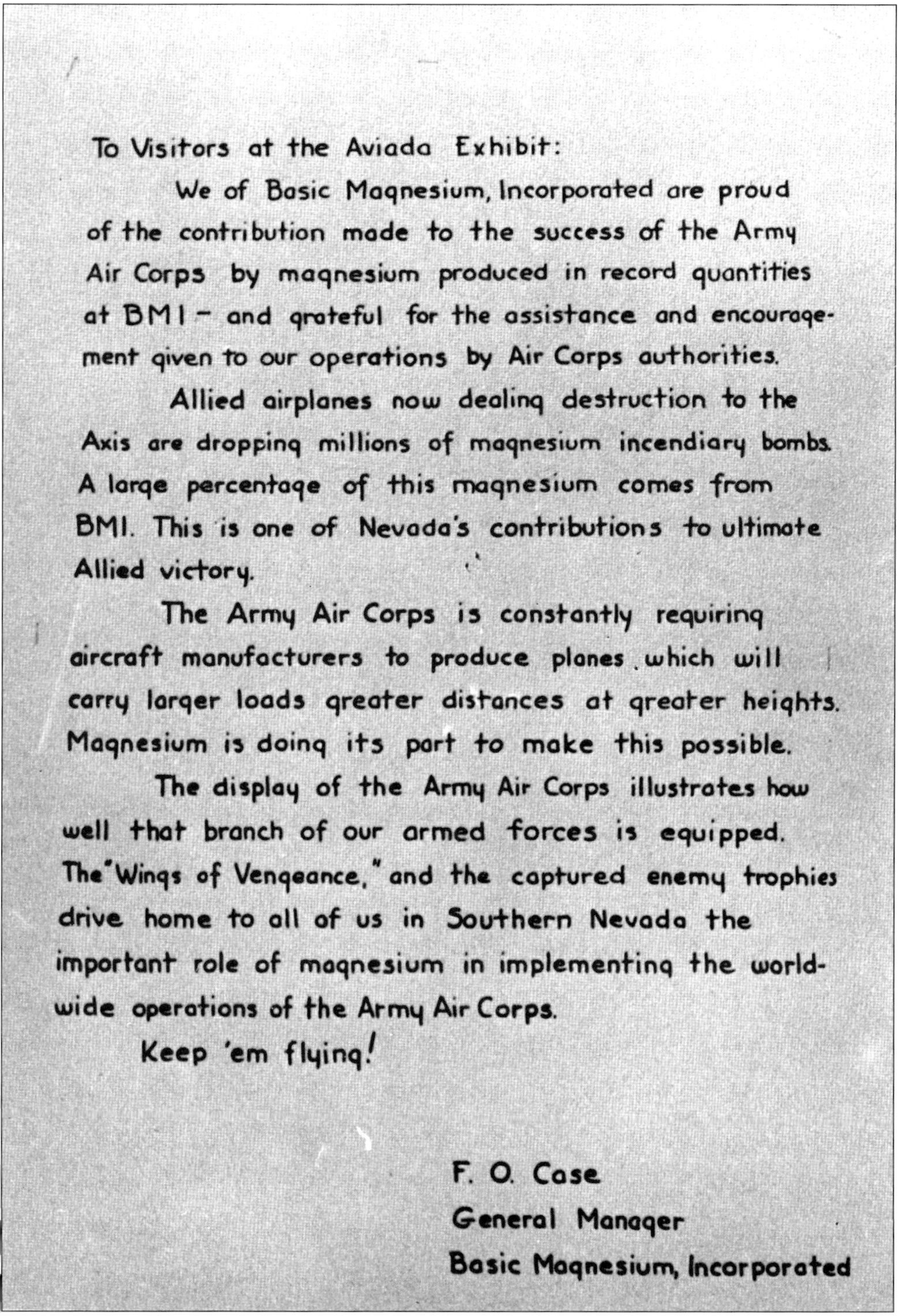

To Visitors at the Aviada Exhibit:

    We of Basic Magnesium, Incorporated are proud of the contribution made to the success of the Army Air Corps by magnesium produced in record quantities at BMI — and grateful for the assistance and encouragement given to our operations by Air Corps authorities.

    Allied airplanes now dealing destruction to the Axis are dropping millions of magnesium incendiary bombs. A large percentage of this magnesium comes from BMI. This is one of Nevada's contributions to ultimate Allied victory.

    The Army Air Corps is constantly requiring aircraft manufacturers to produce planes which will carry larger loads greater distances at greater heights. Magnesium is doing its part to make this possible.

    The display of the Army Air Corps illustrates how well that branch of our armed forces is equipped. The "Wings of Vengeance," and the captured enemy trophies drive home to all of us in Southern Nevada the important role of magnesium in implementing the worldwide operations of the Army Air Corps.

    Keep 'em flying!

                                      F. O. Case
                                      General Manager
                                      Basic Magnesium, Incorporated

DETAIL SHOWING BMI GENERAL MANAGER'S LETTER TO AVIADA EXHIBIT VISITORS, APRIL 15, 1944. Enlarged from the previous photograph, this is F.O. Case's message to exhibit visitors in southern Nevada.

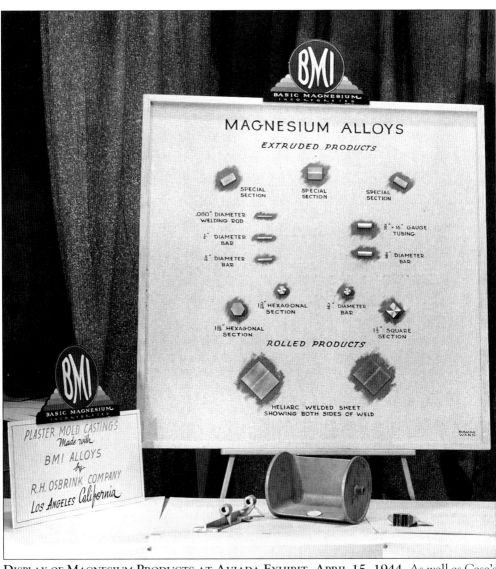

DISPLAY OF MAGNESIUM PRODUCTS AT AVIADA EXHIBIT, APRIL 15, 1944. As well as Case's message, a small display of BMI alloy products was added to the southern Nevada display of the exhibit.

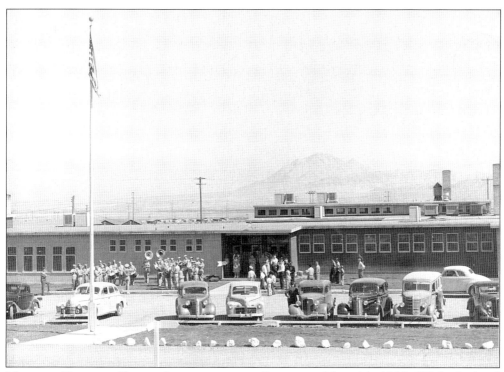

Military Band at Plant Administration Building, May 14, 1944. While the band salutes the plant and all seems prosperous, it is just a few weeks since the federal government started to slow the production of magnesium.

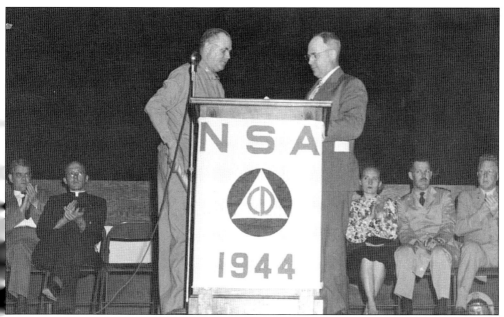

Presentation of National Security Certificate, July 12, 1944. Colonel J.W. Leedom, Senior Field Representative, Protection Services Division, Ninth Region, O.C.D., presents the Certificate of National Security Award to F.O. Case, General Manager, Basic Magnesium Inc.

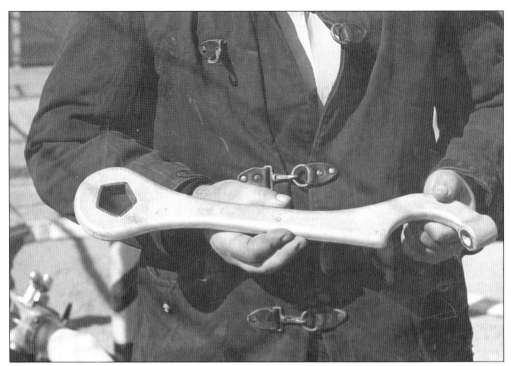

FIREMAN HOLDING MAGNESIUM FIRE HYDRANT WRENCH, OCTOBER 14, 1944. With stockpiles of magnesium beyond any projected need, there are only a few weeks of magnesium production left at the plant. There are peacetime products that can be made from magnesium, but not a need that justifies a plant on this scale.

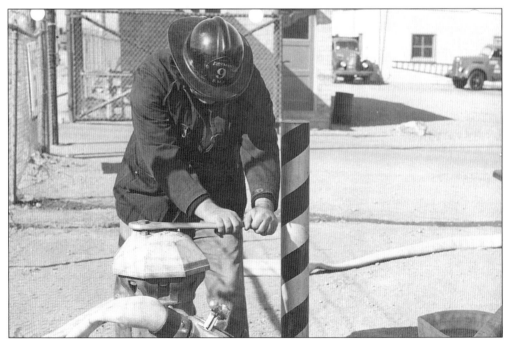

FIREMAN DEMONSTRATING MAGNESIUM FIRE HYDRANT WRENCH, OCTOBER 14, 1944.

Three
LIVING AT THE PLANT

In 1940 Las Vegas was a town of about 8,500 people. At the height of construction in July 1942 the plant employed around 13,000 workers (equal to 10 percent of the state's population!). Where were they and their families to live? Even using every possibility for accommodation in Las Vegas, Pittman, and Boulder City, there were thousands left to house. A commercially run camp and then trailer park gave some relief. However, there was really no choice but for the plant to get into the business of providing housing and all the other necessities that supported a community.

There was resistance to this. Many in Las Vegas thought that the city should be allowed to grow to meet the demand. But just as when the dam was constructed a few years previously, there was federal reluctance to see Las Vegas as a suitable place for reliable workers to live. The housing needs of the dam project had led to the founding of Boulder City. Informal action by entrepreneurs and project workers had led to the development of Midway City (Pittman) between Boulder City and Las Vegas.

With wartime controls, there was not the same possibility for private development, but the federal government did not want to found another town. The housing that was provided for thousands of BMI families was asserted to be temporary. The federal government assured Las Vegas that it would be dismantled and removed after the need had passed.

And so streets and homes appeared in the desert with each new development looking more permanent than the last.

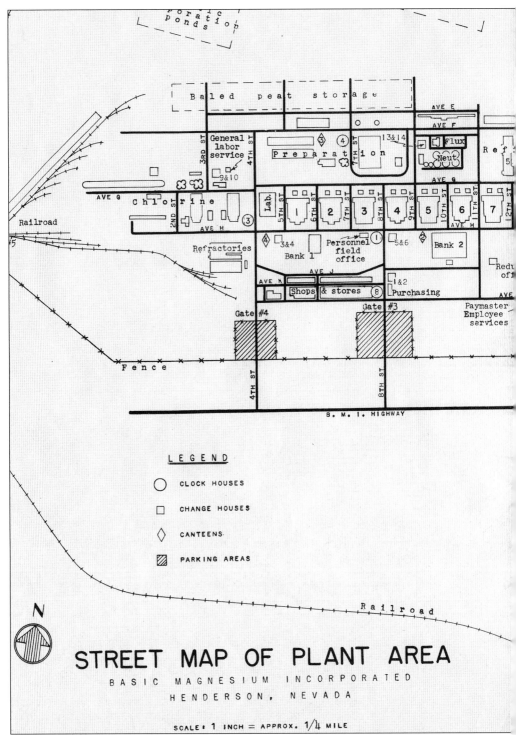

STREET MAP OF PLANT AREA, 1944. This map of the plant and its surroundings was published in January 1944. The area at the lower right between Boulder Highway and the railroad is Basic Townsite (already called Henderson on this map). Victory Village is just across Boulder

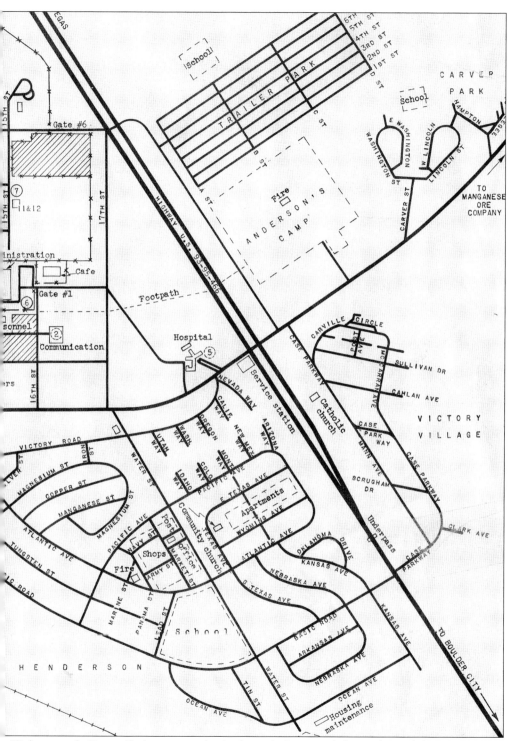

Highway with Carver Park to its north. Anderson's Camp and the trailer park between Carver Park and the highway complete the residential areas. The dead-end BMI Highway on this map is now the major thoroughfare of Lake Mead Drive.

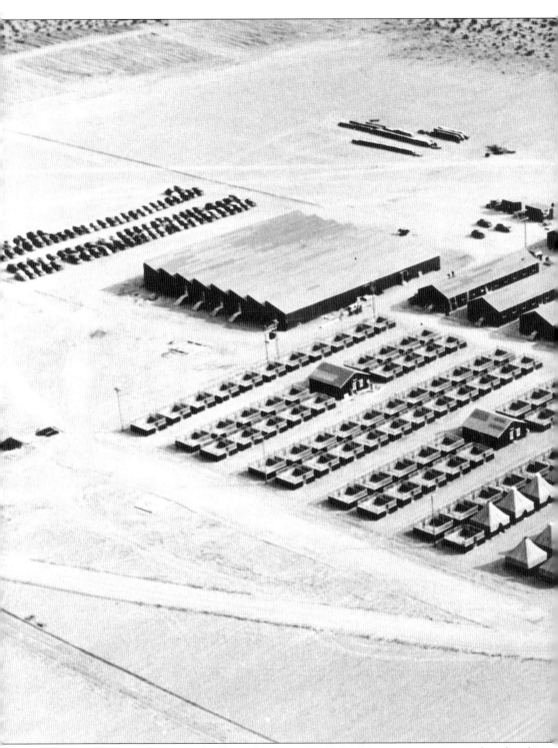

AERIAL VIEW OF ANDERSON'S CAMP, JANUARY 5, 1942. Many construction workers lived in Las Vegas, but there was nowhere near enough extra housing available in what was then a small town. Some workers had to live in their cars in the desert and the winter of 1941–1942 was

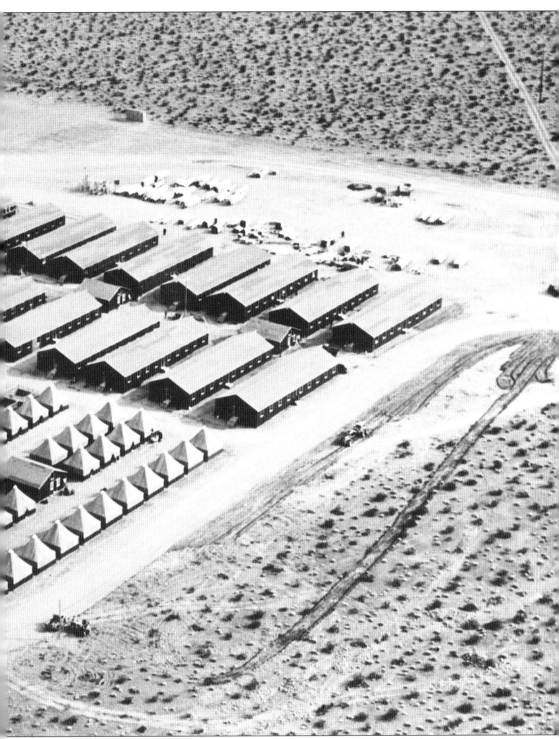

bitterly cold. The first reasonable housing at the plant was the camp established by Anderson Supply Company of Las Vegas. This provided both tents and barrack style accommodations. The barracks had the advantage of evaporative coolers for the summer.

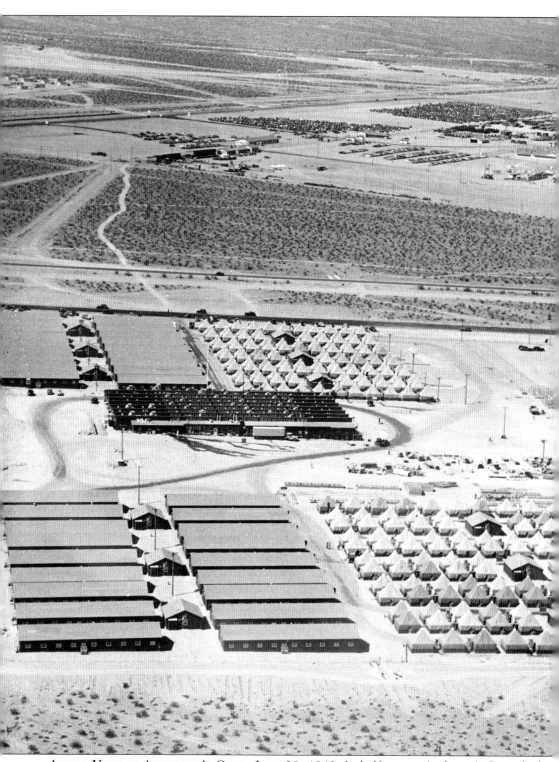
AERIAL VIEW OF ANDERSON'S CAMP, JULY 28, 1942. In half a year, Anderson's Camp had grown considerably—as had the plant which can be seen rising across Boulder Highway.

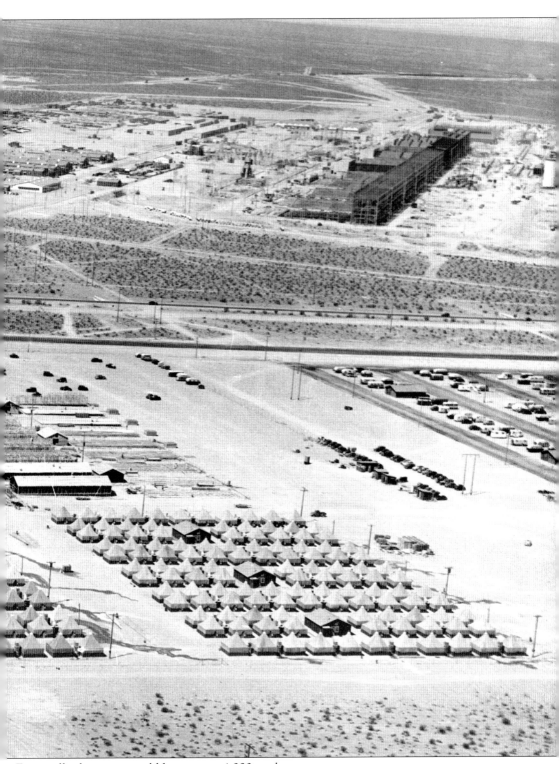

Eventually the camp would house over 4,000 workers.

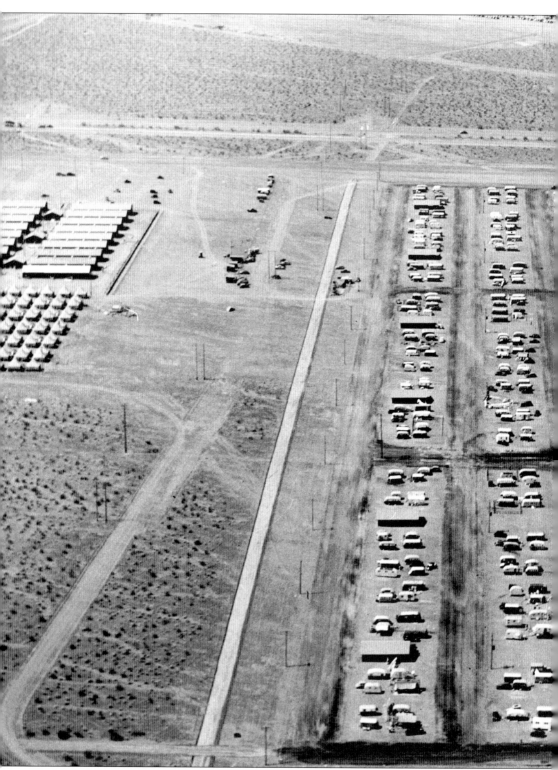

AERIAL VIEW OF THE TRAILER PARK, AUGUST 11, 1942. Just north of Anderson's Camp was

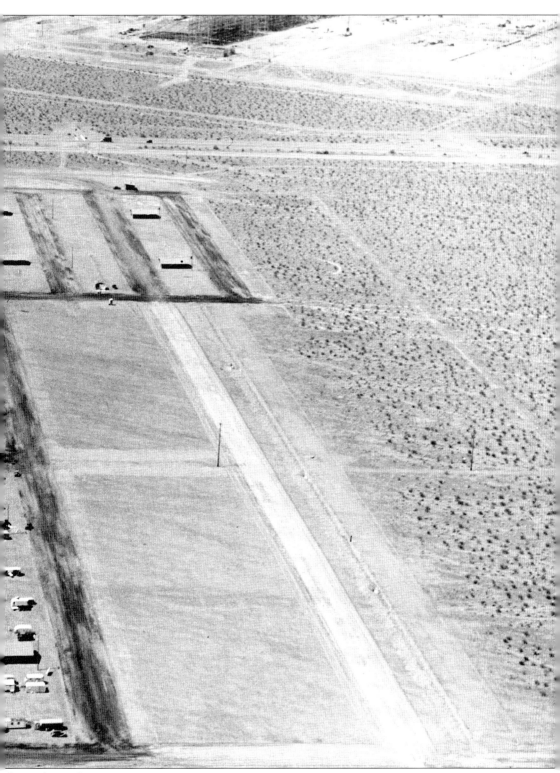
the trailer park.

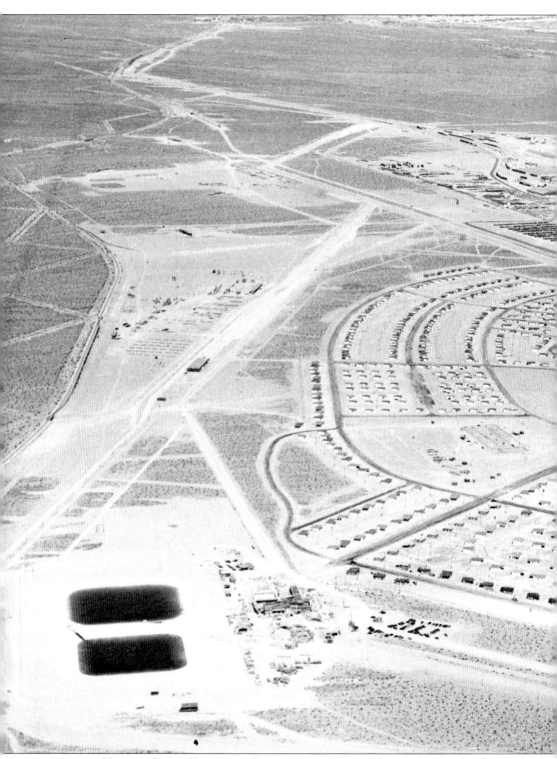

AERIAL VIEW OF BASIC TOWNSITE, JULY 28, 1942. Even if it was supposed to be temporary housing like Anderson's Camp and the Trailer Park, Basic Townsite looked much more like a

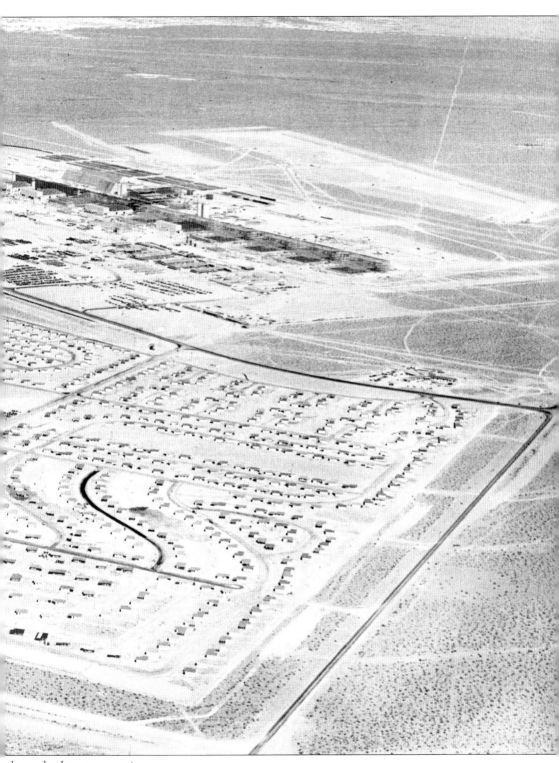
planned urban community.

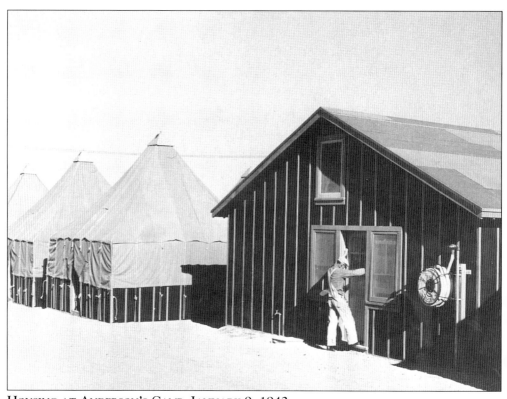
Housing at Anderson's Camp, January 9, 1942.

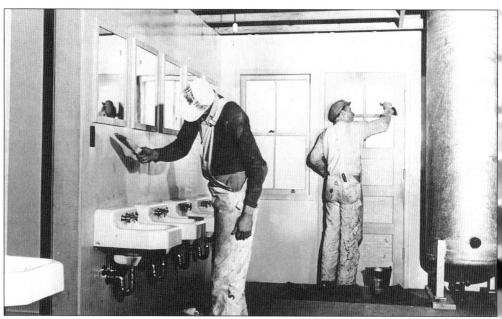
Painting Bathroom at Anderson's Camp, January 9, 1942.

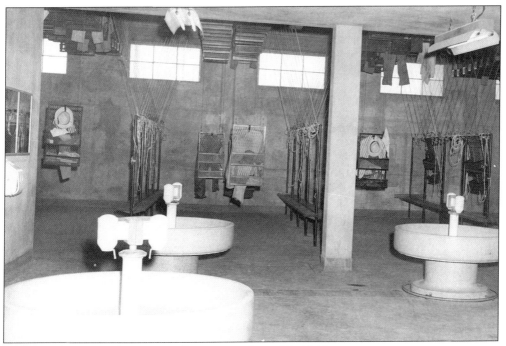

ANOTHER STYLE OF COMMUNAL BATHROOM JULY 10, 1943.

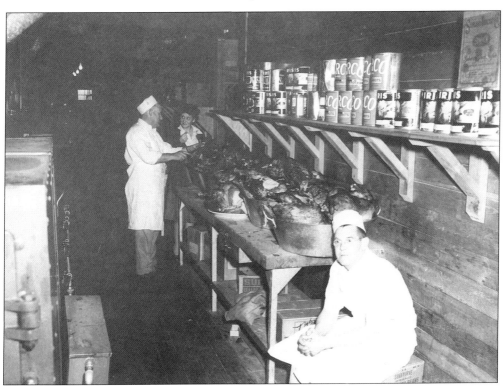

CAMP KITCHEN, NOVEMBER 25, 1942. The camp cafeteria could provide up to 20,000 meals a day, prepared and served by up to 200 employees.

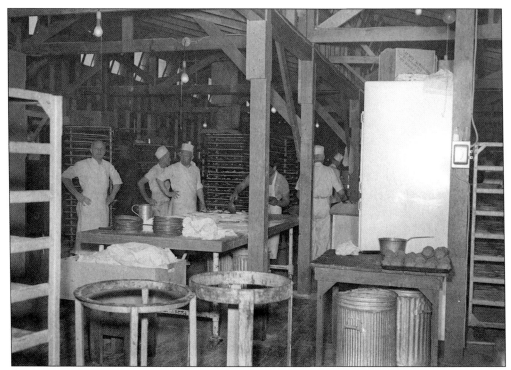

CAMP KITCHEN, FEBRUARY 17, 1943.

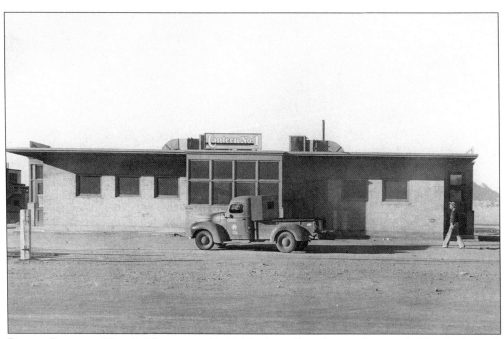

PLANT CANTEEN NO. 1, NOVEMBER 2, 1943. As well as the meals provided by Anderson's and at homes, there were several canteens in the plant itself.

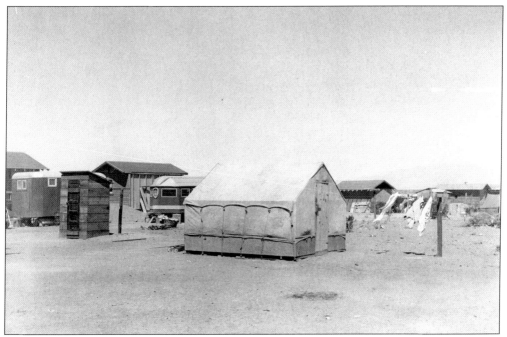

HOUSING AT TRAILER PARK, APRIL 18, 1942. While the facilities at Anderson's Camp may not have been luxurious, the trailer park next door may have made them seem quite acceptable. The trailer park bathroom provisions certainly lacked more than a coat of paint.

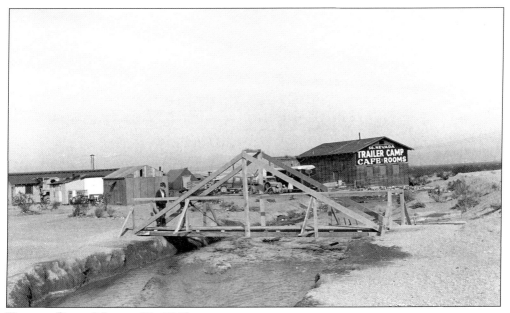

TRAILER PARK, MARCH 13, 1943.

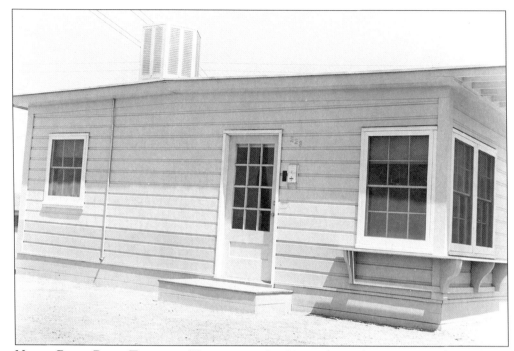

NEWLY BUILT BASIC TOWNSITE HOME, 1942. Las Vegas objected to permanent homes being built at the plant as wartime building restrictions limited home building in overcrowded Las Vegas. The compromise was that Las Vegas would be allowed to issue 1,000 home building permits and 1,000 "demountable" houses would be built at the plant to be removed after the war. In fact, many are still lived in today.

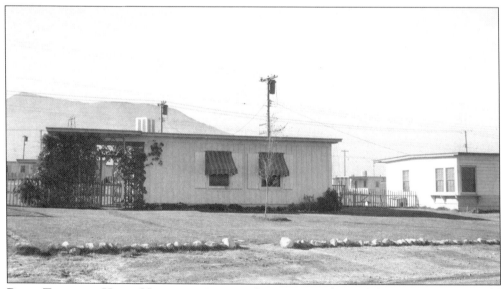

BASIC TOWNSITE HOME, NOVEMBER 3, 1943. Some new residents of the manufactured homes set about giving them a more custom look.

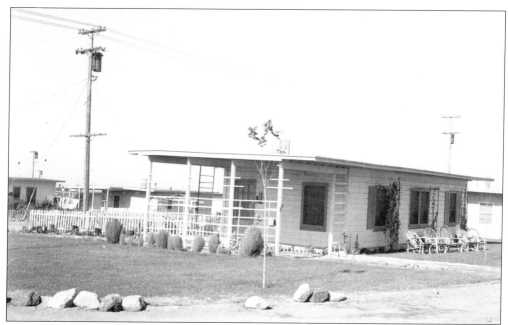
Basic Townsite Home, November 2, 1943.

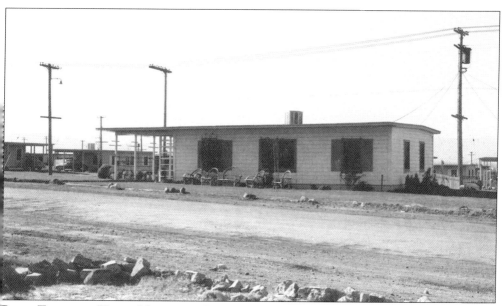
Basic Townsite Home, November 3, 1943.

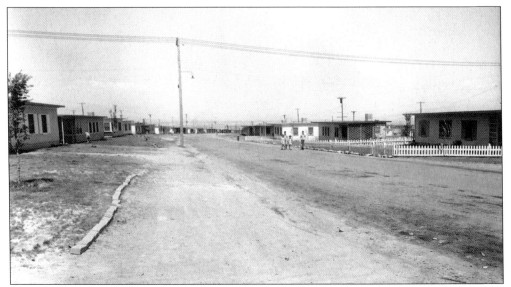

A TOWNSITE NEIGHBORHOOD, MAY 21, 1943.

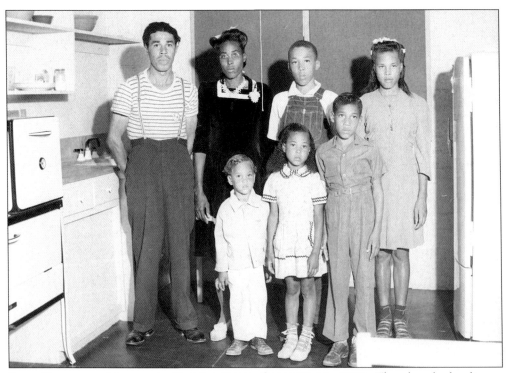

FIRST FAMILY TO MOVE INTO CARVER PARK, OCTOBER 13, 1943. The plant had a diverse workforce, but there was also segregation. Carver Park was built to house African-American workers with 64 dormitory units for unmarried workers, 104 one-bedroom, 104 two-bedroom, and 52 three-bedroom apartments. In addition, there was to be an athletic field, recreation hall, and school. This photo shows the first family to move into a new home there. Pictured left to right are: (front row) Yvonne (3), Clarice (5), Roscoe (9); (back row) Robert C. Williams, Rosie Lee Williams, Theodore (14), and Cleopatra (13).

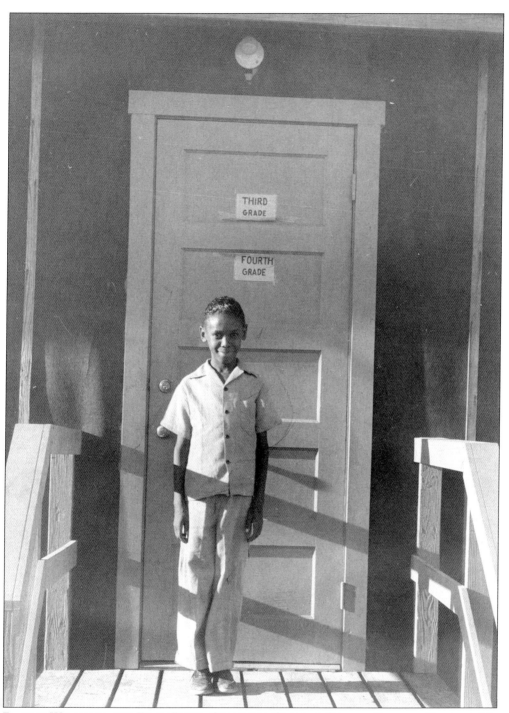

ROSCOE WILLIAMS, THE FIRST PUPIL, STANDING OUTSIDE CARVER SCHOOL, OCTOBER 13, 1943. Most African-American plant workers continued to live in Las Vegas and Carver Park and its school was never fully occupied as intended.

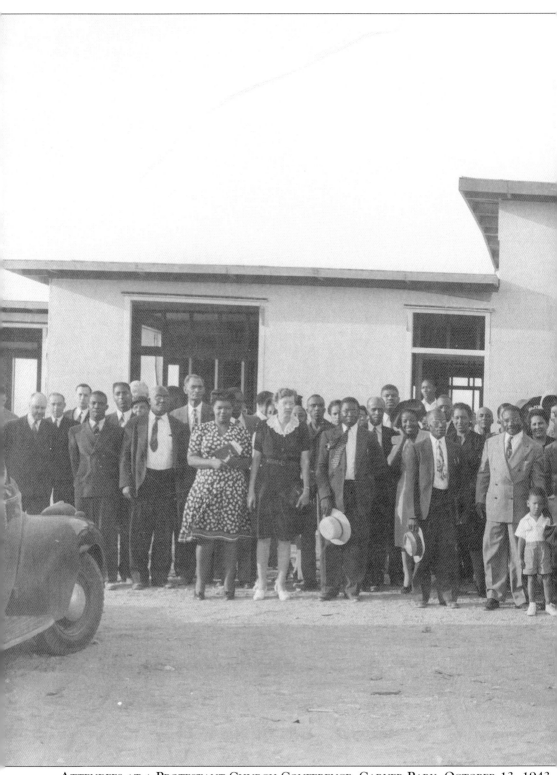
Attendees at a Protestant Church Conference, Carver Park, October 13, 1943.

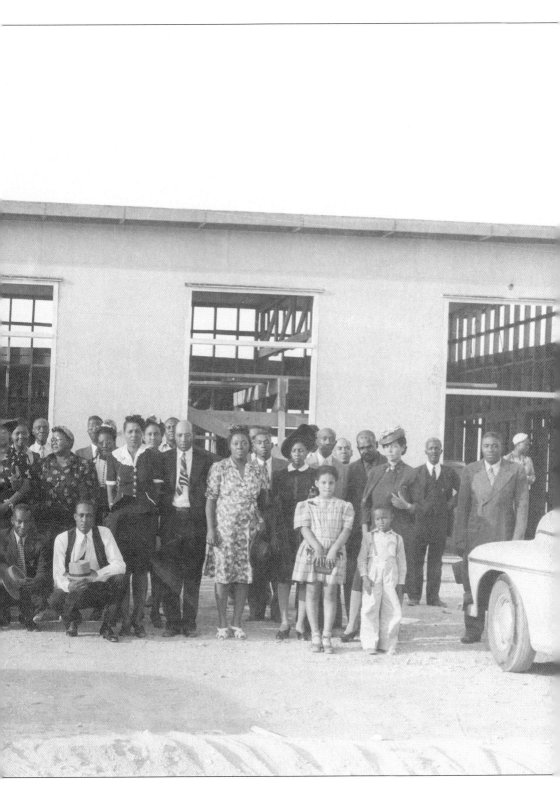

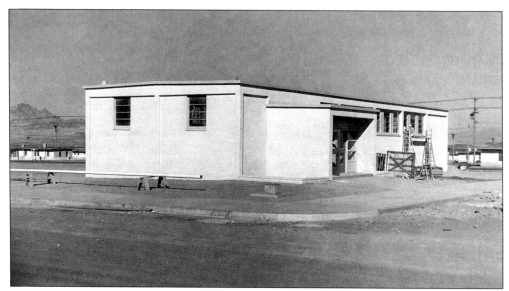

PUTTING THE FINISHING TOUCHES TO THE POST OFFICE, NOVEMBER 29, 1943. When the new post office was dedicated on January 10, 1944, it was named after former Senator Charles B. Henderson, giving Basic Townsite a new name that would later extend to a new city. Henderson was chairman of the Reconstruction Finance Corporation, which financed building the plant.

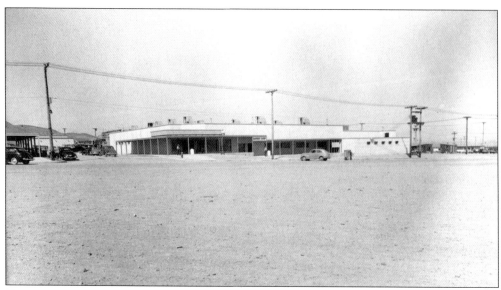

THE DRUGSTORE MAY 21, 1943. Just to the left of the utility pole in the middle of this commercial block is the Barber Shop's sign.

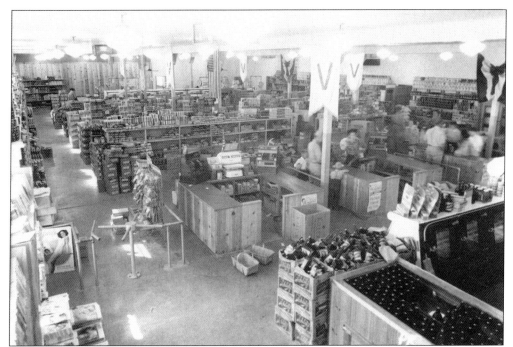

INSIDE THE TOWNSITE MARKET, MAY 21, 1943. The staff and customers are a blur of movement at the checkouts in this well-stocked store. The rather racy looking picture of the woman in a swimsuit to the left of the turnstile is a cigarette ad. The federal government prohibited slot machines in the store, but it stocked plenty of beer along with all the household staples.

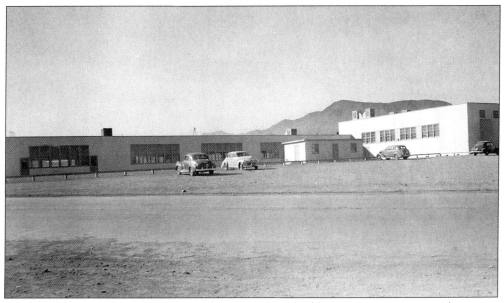

SCHOOL, NOVEMBER 3, 1943. This is the main school building in Basic Townsite. There were also small school buildings in Carver Park and north of the trailer park.

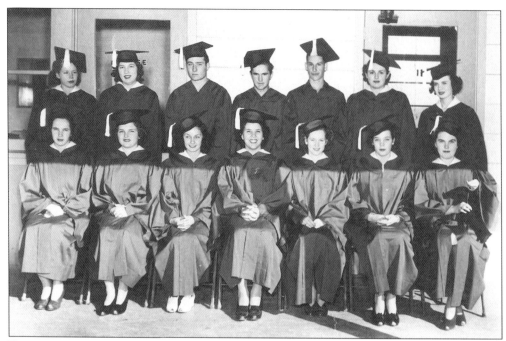

FIRST HIGH SCHOOL GRADUATING CLASS, 1943. The high school opened in October 1942 and had 242 students that year. The school graduated its first class in 1943. Pictured left to right are: (front row) Mary Kelley, Wanda Saunders, Georgia Consalva, Very Keeney, Doris Stransky, Virginia Fallis, and Betty Albin; (back row) Betty Wandell, Aldis Schmidt, Alan McCullum, William McPhee, William Bedwell, Annabelle Plunkett, and Marjorie Bertolini. Also graduating, but not in the photograph, were Dale Johnson and Dean Johnson.

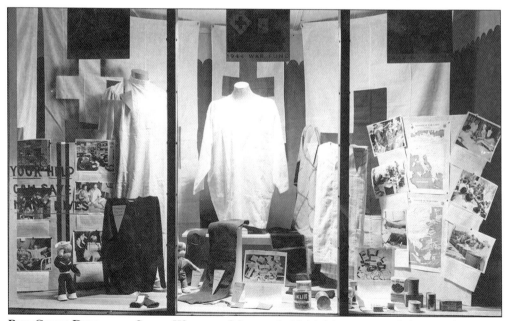

RED CROSS DISPLAY IN STORE WINDOW, MARCH 4, 1944. Many wives of plant workers were active in the local Red Cross.

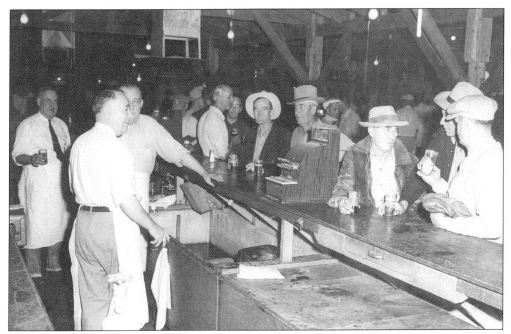

BAR INTERIOR. The tough working conditions at the plant produced a demand for places to relax such as this makeshift bar.

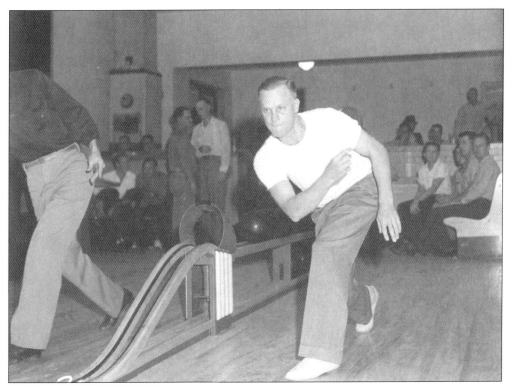

MEN BOWLING, SEPTEMBER 28, 1943. While the local bars may have had something of the Old West about them, this bowling alley and its patrons look much more modern.

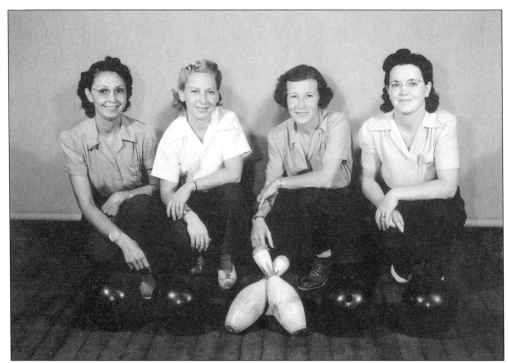

WOMEN BOWLERS, AUGUST 19, 1944. Women, whether they worked at the plant, in local businesses, or at home, also needed their recreation.

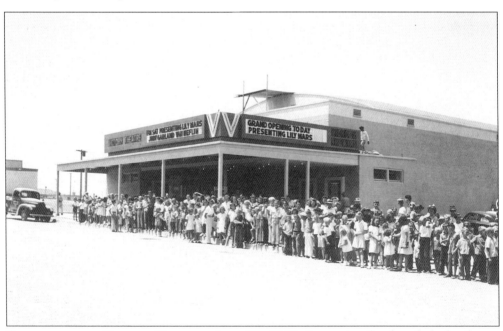

OPENING OF THE VICTORY THEATRE, JULY 22, 1943. Recreation for the whole family was available with the opening of a movie theater. In 1954, as the company town was transforming into a self-sufficient city, this theater would install a new screen, 21 feet by 43 feet, then claimed to be the largest movie screen in the state.

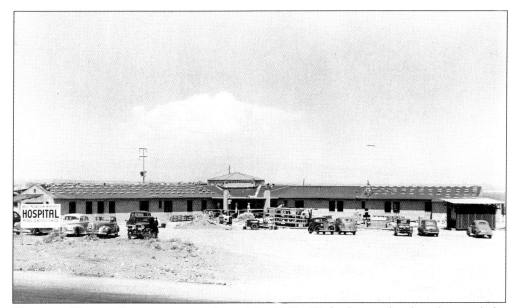

HOSPITAL UNDER CONSTRUCTION, JULY 23, 1942. With thousands of workers and the dangers of the construction site and plant operation, there was a need for nearby medical services. The hospital was operated as a federal facility until 1947 when the Adrian Dominican Sisters of Michigan purchased the hospital for $1, but also assumed its debt. It was renamed Rose de Lima (later St. Rose de Lima, and then St. Rose Dominican) Hospital and in 1955 became the first hospital in southern Nevada to be accredited by the Joint Commission of Accreditation of Hospitals.

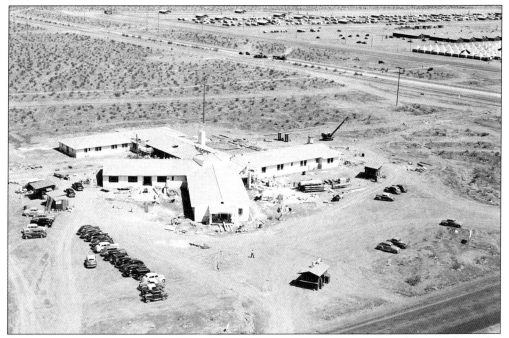

AERIAL VIEW OF HOSPITAL UNDER CONSTRUCTION, AUGUST 11, 1942. This view shows the radial construction of the hospital.

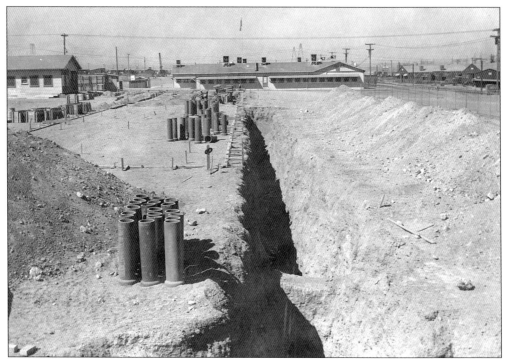

LAYING SEWER PIPES, APRIL 2, 1943. It might not be a popular topic for conversation, but one of the most basic needs any community must meet is to provide for the safe disposal of waste. Among the many infrastructure expenses to building the plant in the desert was creating a sewage disposal system from scratch. A very practical reason why Las Vegas could not accommodate all the plant workers, even if the city had been allowed to build enough housing, was that the city sewer system could not have coped with such an increase in use.

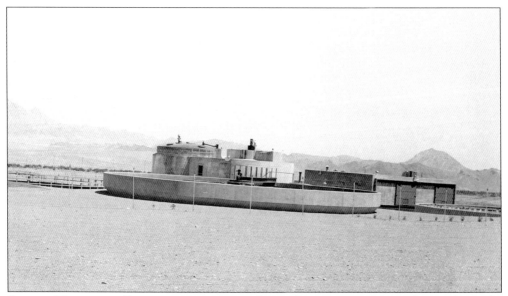

SEWAGE TREATMENT PLANT, MAY 21, 1943. Ironically, given sanitary conditions there, the sewage treatment plant was located just north of the trailer park.

Four
FOUNDING A CITY

Henderson incorporated as a city in the spring of 1953. By November 1954, the local newspaper was claiming that Henderson must be the fastest growing city in the United States as the population had increased by over 100 percent in the preceding 18 months. Henderson has been growth-oriented from its beginning, even if growth usually outstripped expectations.

The city started with high hopes. BMI stayed outside the boundaries of the incorporated city but it donated the physical plant it had operated for such infrastructure as water and sewers. The city boldly claimed a debt-free management policy. However, reality quickly set in and the Mayor and Council had to explain to the citizens that much of the city's physical infrastructure was aging and required expensive maintenance work and upgrading. In addition, Clark County informed the new city that county police service would cease on July 1, 1953. Henderson had to establish its own police. A loan from the state was needed to help the city stay in business.

As the financial realities of running a city hit home and were dealt with, community life and civic identity developed and the economic and social institutions that make up city life were being reinforced and created.

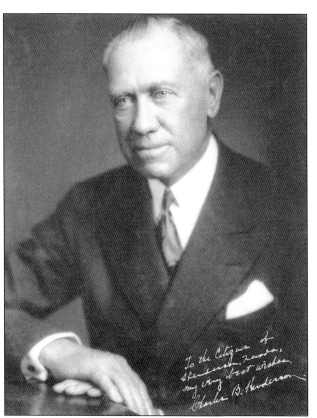

SENATOR CHARLES B. HENDERSON. At the request of the mayor, the former Nevada senator sent this photograph to the newly founded city which had taken his name. The inscription reads: "To the Citizens of Henderson, Nevada, my very best wishes. Charles B. Henderson."

JUDGE HENDERSON SWEARS IN CITY COUNCIL, MAY 27, 1953. Pictured left to right are: Judge Albert S. Henderson; Paul Dickover, Ward 5; Lou LaPorta, Ward 3; John Ivary, Ward 2; Bill Engel, Ward 4; and N.D. Van Wagenan, Ward 1.

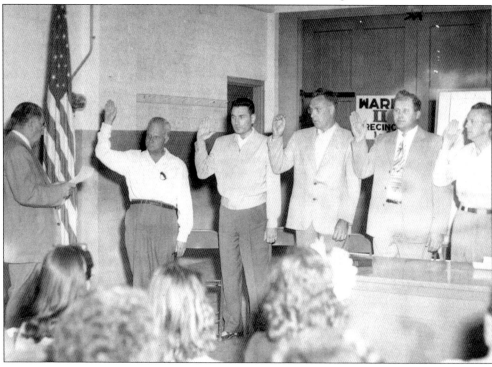

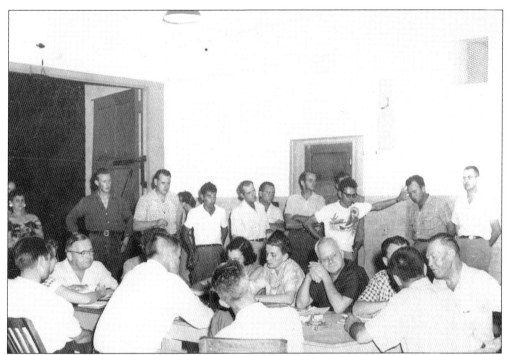

FIRST OFFICIAL TOWN MEETING, JUNE 24, 1953. The first official town meeting of the newly incorporated city took place in the high school auditorium. At this meeting citizens started to learn the realities of running their own city.

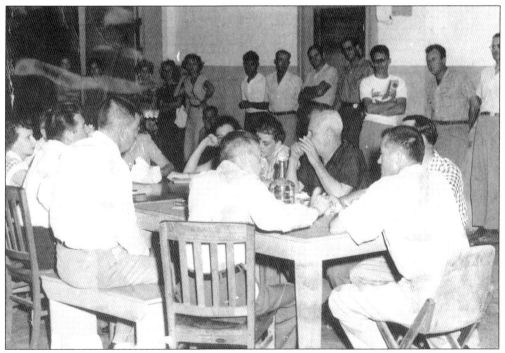

FIRST OFFICIAL TOWN MEETING, JUNE 24, 1953.

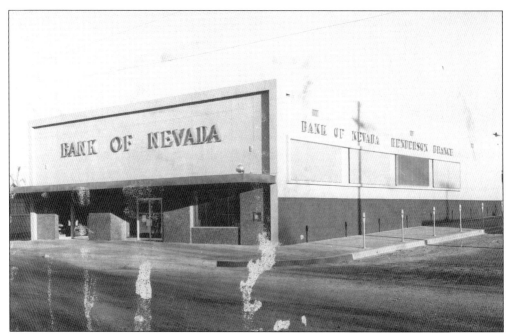

BANK OF NEVADA, HENDERSON BRANCH 1954. A boost to the economic life of the city came with the opening of a local branch of the Bank of Nevada at 7 W. Pacific on February 8, 1954. This impressive new bank was built at a cost of $150,000 and managed by Colvin S. "Bus" Smith Jr.

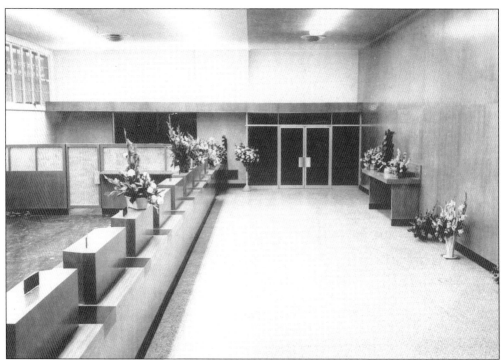

BANK OF NEVADA, HENDERSON BRANCH, INTERIOR, 1954.

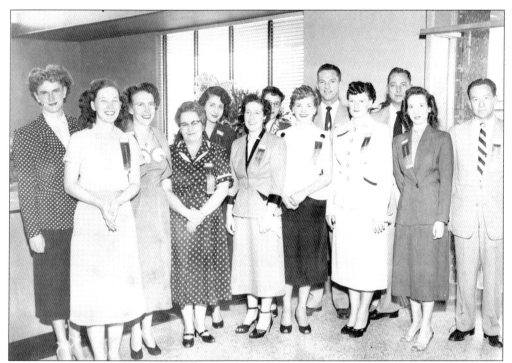

BANK OF NEVADA, HENDERSON BRANCH, EMPLOYEES, 1954. Pictured left to right are: (front row) Mary Gardner, Ellen Hunt, Marjorie Bourke, Althea Dix, Jane McAllister, Bernice Reed, Glennis Hughes, Shirley Dolan, and Frank Pearson (assistant cashier); (back row) Marilyn Pearson, Virginia Brahn, Colvin S. Smith (manager), and Jim Hynney.

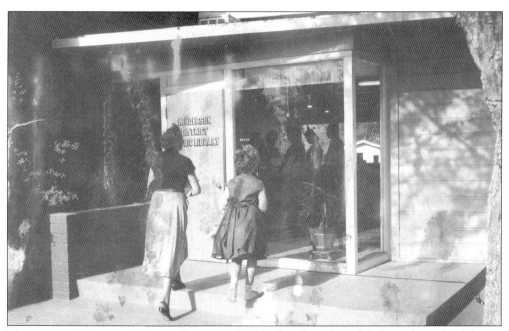

HENDERSON DISTRICT PUBLIC LIBRARY, 1954. Another sign of independent city life was Henderson's own library, which would soon undergo a needed expansion.

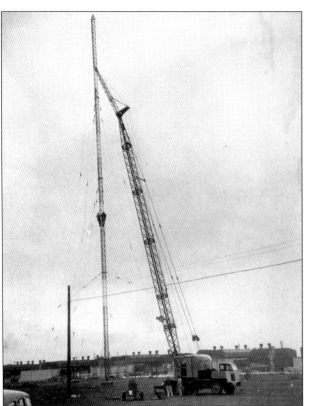

ERECTING KBMI TOWER, 1954. At 12:01 a.m. on Thursday March 11, 1954, KBMI began 24-hour broadcasting of popular music such as Glenn Miller and Tommy Dorsey. The station was owned by Morry Zenoff, owner of the Henderson *Home News*.

GOVERNOR RUSSELL MAKING FIRST DIRECT DIAL CALL, APRIL 1, 1954. At 7:00 p.m. on Thursday, April 1, 1954, Henderson switched over to a new $300,000 direct dial telephone system. Governor Charles Russell made the first call on the system. As the switchover involved the phones going dead for about 10 minutes, the call was to Morry Zenoff at KBMI and was broadcast live to let everyone know the phones were in business again.

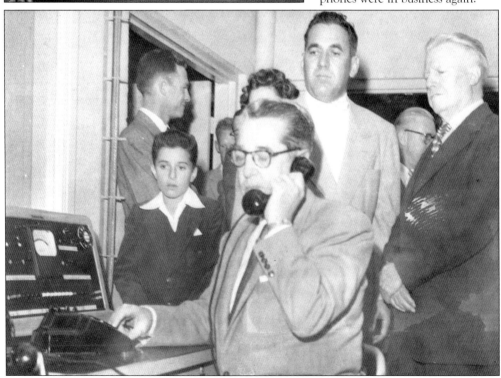

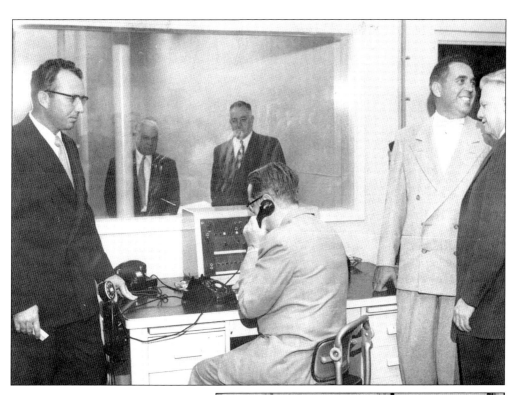

GOVERNOR RUSSELL MAKING FIRST DIRECT DIAL CALL, APRIL 1, 1954. Pictured here, left to right, are: (foreground) Herschel Trumbo, president of Henderson Telephone Co.; Governor Charles Russell; W.J. Urga, secretary and treasurer of Henderson Telephone Co.; and Robert Allen, chairman of the Nevada Public Services Commission. The men behind the glass are unidentified.

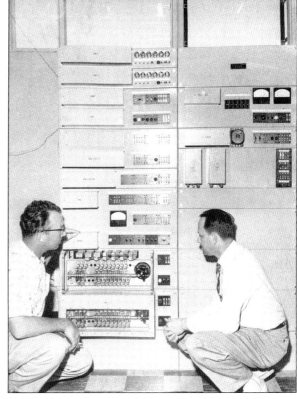

HERSCHEL TRUMBO AND INSTALLING ENGINEER WITH PANEL FOR NEW TELEPHONE SYSTEM 1954.

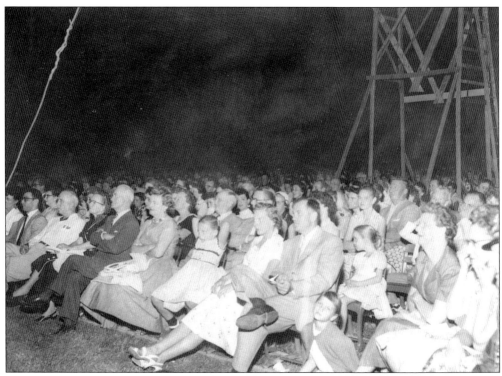

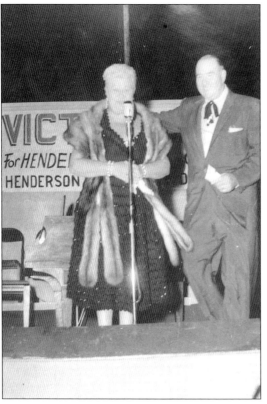

SOME OF THE AUDIENCE AT THE YOUTH CENTER VICTORY SHOW FUNDRAISER, JUNE 14, 1954. The building of a youth center to provide recreational activities brought together the whole city and demonstrated what they could accomplish. The city and the school board split the salary for a recreation director; BMI donated the land; the VFW, Lions Club, and Henderson Police held fundraisers; businesses and citizens donated money, materials, and labor. The largest fund raising event was the Victory Show held in a huge tent erected at the Ben Church Memorial Field. Many Las Vegas entertainers performed at this event, which raised nearly $10,000.

SOPHIE TUCKER AT YOUTH CENTER VICTORY SHOW FUNDRAISER, JUNE 14, 1954. Sophie Tucker, singer and movie star, is pictured here with Abe Schiller, one of the evening's MCs. She presented a check for $100 and pledged $100 each month until the Youth Center was built.

Frank Sinatra Performing at Youth Center Victory Show Fundraiser, June 14, 1954.

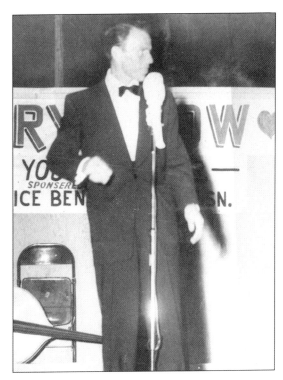

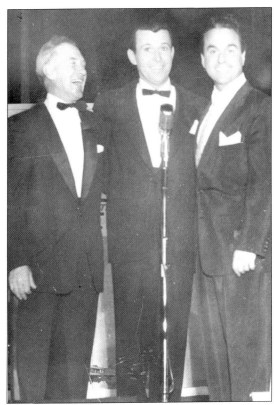

Youth Center Victory Show Fundraiser, June 14, 1954. Pictured left to right are: Harry White, producer of the show; Dennis Day, entertainer; and Stan Irwin, one of the evening's MCs.

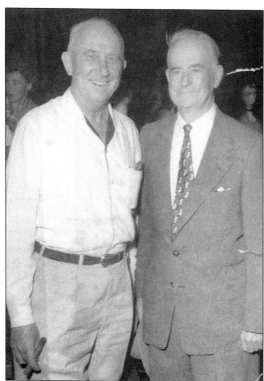

Las Vegas Mayor C.D. Baker and Former Nevada Governor Vail Pittman at Youth Center Victory Show Fundraiser, June 14, 1954.

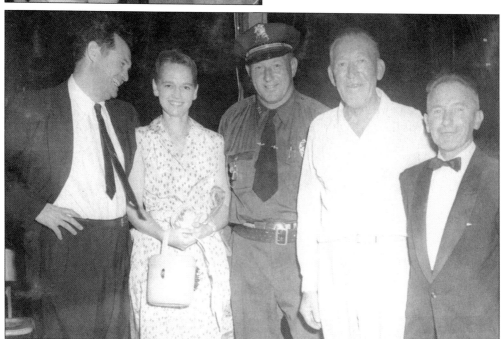

At Youth Center Victory Show Fundraiser, June 14, 1954. Pictured left to right are: Hank Greenspun, editor of the *Las Vegas Sun*; Dorothy (Dottie) McBeath, chairman of the Henderson Recreation Board; George Crisler, Henderson chief of police; Fay Hammond, talent and liaison; and Harry White, variety president and producer of the show.

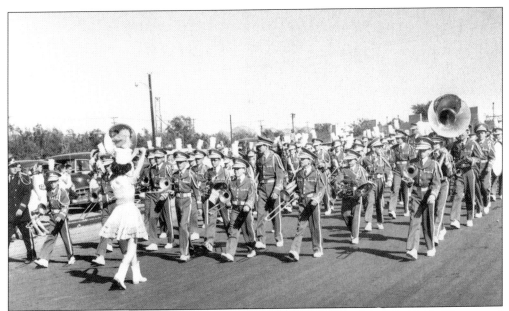

HIGH SCHOOL MARCHING BAND IN INDUSTRIAL DAYS PARADE, MAY 7, 1955. The annual Industrial Days celebrated Henderson's heritage with a parade, special events, and a published program featuring local history.

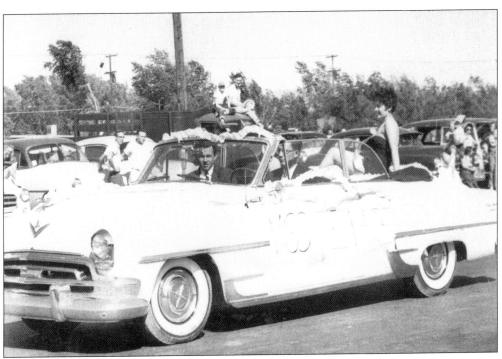

"MISS TEENAGE" IN INDUSTRIAL DAYS PARADE, MAY 7, 1955.

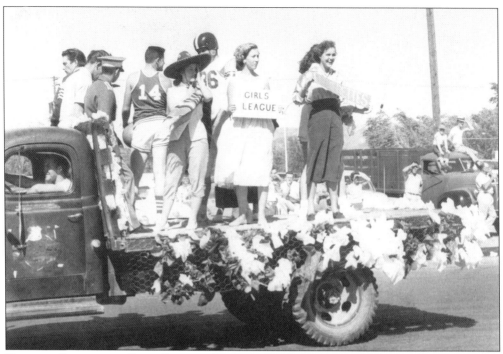

FLOAT IN INDUSTRIAL DAYS PARADE, MAY 7, 1955.

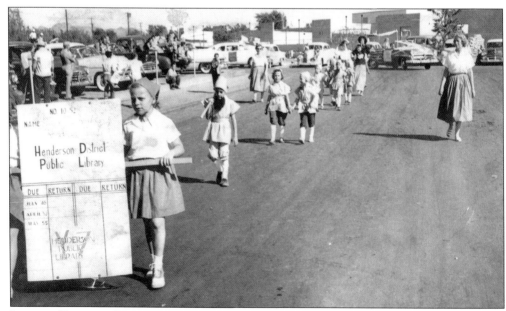

LIBRARY ENTRY IN INDUSTRIAL DAYS PARADE, MAY 7, 1955. The oversized library checkout card is followed by children dressed as Snow White and the seven dwarfs.

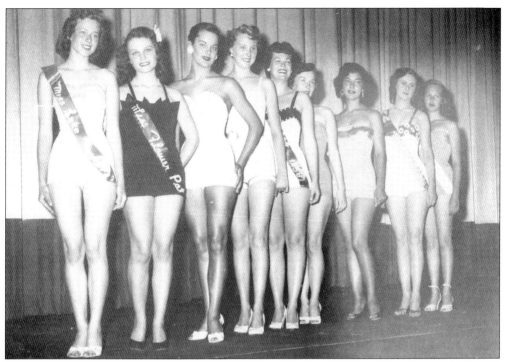

BEAUTY PAGEANT CONTESTANTS FROM INDUSTRIAL DAYS, MAY 1955.

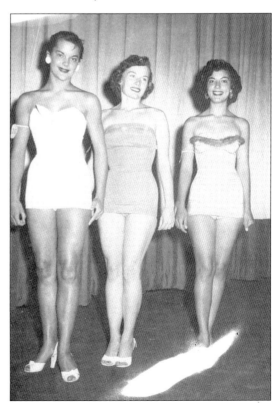

BEAUTY PAGEANT WINNERS FROM INDUSTRIAL DAYS, MAY 1955. Pictured left to right are: 1st Marilyn Spellman; 2nd Donna Bogut; and 3rd Zeke Marino.

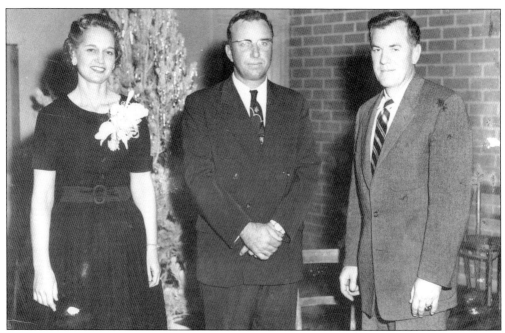

SOME MEMBERS OF YOUTH CENTER BUILDING COMMITTEE, DECEMBER 29, 1957. Pictured left to right are: Dottie McBeath, vice-president; Herschel Trumbo, president; and Dr. James French, mayor of Henderson. Also on the committee were Dave Jamison, secretary; Colvin Smith Jr., treasurer; A.T. Newell; Frank Schreck; Frank Broncfield; Earl Keenan; Bill Mainor; Chet Sewell; and Georgia Weese.

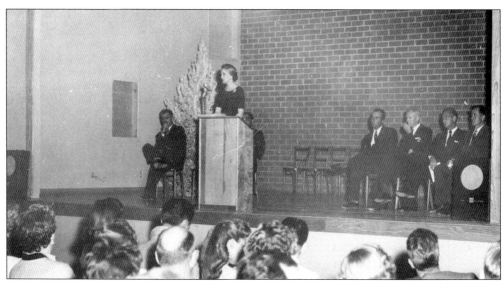

DEDICATION OF YOUTH CENTER BUILDING, DECEMBER 29, 1957. Dottie McBeath speaks at the ceremony turning the completed Youth Center over to the city, free of debt. Building this center and its adjoining swimming pool was a major achievement for the community and showed how transforming Henderson from a company town to a city dedicated to the needs of its residents required not just incorporation and a city government but the active participation of the residents themselves.

AFTERWORD

When was Henderson Incorporated?

Every place has its myths and misconceptions about its past, and Henderson is no exception. For example, there is the myth that before BMI nobody in the United States knew how to make magnesium. But one thing seems like it should be a simple question of fact—What date marks the incorporation of the city? For many years, the date of June 8, 1953, was used. It even appeared on city seals. Yet, as we will see, this was one of the less substantive dates in the process.

As was required by state law, the formal process of incorporating the city began March 27, 1953, with the collecting of signatures of qualified electors and tax-payers on a petition applying for incorporation of a specified area of Clark County with the proposed name of Henderson. This petition was submitted to the District Court with the other required papers. On April 16, 1953, Judge Albert S. Henderson issued a decree declaring the City of Henderson "duly incorporated."

Judge Henderson's decree named five commissioners to call an election, with thirty days notice, for a mayor and five councilmen. The commissioners were to report the results of the election to the court, and the clerk of the court was to certify the results. When the commissioners had completed their duties, they were to be paid $75 each by the city.

The minutes of the initial meeting of the election commissioners on April 18 state that they are meeting "In pursuance of a decree . . . declaring the City of Henderson duly Incorporated." On April 23 the commissioners had a Notice of Election for Saturday May 23 posted in five places and published in the *Henderson Home News*. The election took place as scheduled and on May 25 the Clerk of the District Court certified the results.

The Commissioners having submitted all the required documents to the Court, on June 4, the Clerk of the Court certified photostatic copies of the court file on the incorporation. As required by law, the Election Commissioners deposited a copy with the new City Clerk, along with the records of the election, as their final official act.

As further required by state law, the Clerk of the Court also sent a copy of the court file to the Secretary of State in Carson City. This was received by the Secretary of State on June 8. To complete the statutory process, the Secretary of State published a "Notice of Incorporation" in the *Nevada Appeal* on June 8, 9, 10, 11, 12, 15, and 16. This served to notify "the people of the State of Nevada . . . of the due incorporation and existence of the City of Henderson" as on June 8 copies of all papers in the office of the Clerk of the Court in respect of this incorporation had been filed with the Secretary of State, and "by virtue of a decree of the . . . Court . . . made and entered on the 16th day of April, 1953, and subsequent proceedings duly had in said Court, the City of Henderson . . . is duly incorporated."

The Secretary of State then issued a "Certificate of Incorporation" on June 17. This certified that the Clerk of the Court had filed copies of the papers on June 8; that notice of the incorporation had been published seven times; and that "the incorporation of the City of Henderson, as a city of the second class, as aforesaid, is now complete."

In the June 18 issue of *Home News*, an article by Mayor French began "By the time this reaches publication, we should have our incorporation complete and be ready to begin operating as a city." It would seem that the Mayor and Council (as advised by the City Attorney) regarded the issuing of the Secretary of State's certificate as necessary to make the incorporation "official" and allow the city administration to act. In fact, state law, repeated in Judge Henderson's decree, provided that the elected officers "shall" organize when the Election Commissioners had filed the records of the incorporation and election with the City Clerk and that this organization was legally effective.

Others understood the incorporation as effective from Judge Henderson's April 16 order. Thus, on February 3, 1956, an article about Henderson in the *Las Vegas Review Journal* referred to "the incorporation of the city in Judge Henderson's court April 1953." However, it would seem that a third point of view predominated from about 1957, and for many years it was customary to refer to the city being incorporated on June 8—the date on which the certified copy of the court file reached the Secretary of State's office.

The 1907 law under which the city incorporated states that a city is "duly incorporated" by the judge's decree, and that the incorporation is "complete" after the publications by the Secretary of State. Yet, the statute also says that judicial notice shall be taken of the elected officials as soon as they organize. So, there seems to be a choice of dates in answer to our seemingly simple question—What date marks the incorporation of the city? April 16, 1953, the city was "duly incorporated" by Court decree. Anytime after June 4, the elected officials could have organized and taken action. June 16 was the final publication that made the incorporation "complete." And June 17 was when the Secretary of State issued his certificate to that effect.